# Recall Tests for GCSE 9–1 Maths

## KS3 knowledge retrieval

**Peter Ransom**

William Collins' dream of knowledge for all began with the publication of his first book in 1819.
A self-educated mill worker, he not only enriched millions of lives, but also founded a flourishing
publishing house. Today, staying true to this spirit, Collins books are packed with inspiration,
innovation and practical expertise. They place you at the centre of a world of possibility
and give you exactly what you need to explore it.

Collins. Freedom to teach.

Collins
An imprint of HarperCollins*Publishers*
The News Building
1 London Bridge Street
London
SE1 9GF

Browse the complete Collins catalogue at **www.collins.co.uk**

© HarperCollins*Publishers* Limited 2018

10 9 8 7 6 5 4 3 2 1

ISBN 978-0-00-831159-9

British Library Cataloguing in Publication Data. A catalogue record for this publication is available from the British Library.

Author: Peter Ransom

Publisher: Katie Sergeant

Senior Editor: Mike Appleton

Editorial packager: Life Lines Editorial Services

Reviewer: Trevor Senior

Cover designer: The Big Mountain Design, Ken Vail Graphic Design

Production controller: Katharine Willard

Printed and bound by CPI Group (UK) Ltd, Croydon, CR0 4YY

# Contents

|  | **Page** |
|---|---|
| **Introduction** | 1 |

**Number**

| | | |
|---|---|---|
| **1** | Understand and use place value for decimals, measures and integers of any size | 2 |
| **2** | Order positive integers, decimals and fractions | 3 |
| **3** | Order negative integers, decimals and fractions | 4 |
| **4** | Use the symbols =, ≠, <, >, ≤, ≥ | 5 |
| **5** | Work with prime numbers and express a number as the product of prime factors | 6 |
| **6** | Work out HCF (highest common factor) of two or more numbers using any method | 7 |
| **7** | Work out LCM (lowest common multiple) of two or more numbers using any method | 8 |
| **8** | Apply the four operations to integers, both positive and negative | 9 |
| **9** | Apply the four operations to decimals, both positive and negative | 10 |
| **10** | Apply + and − to simple fractions (including improper fractions and mixed numbers), both positive and negative | 11 |
| **11** | Apply × and ÷ to simple fractions, (including improper fractions and mixed numbers), both positive and negative | 12 |
| **12** | Use conventional notation for priority of operations, including brackets, powers, roots and reciprocals | 13 |
| **13** | Use positive integer powers and associated real roots (square, cube and higher) | 14 |
| **14** | Recognise powers of 2, 3, 4, 5 | 15 |
| **15** | Distinguish between exact representations of roots and their decimal approximations | 16 |
| **16** | Interpret and compare numbers in standard form $A \times 10^n$ (where n is an integer) | 17 |
| **17** | Work interchangeably with terminating decimals and their corresponding fractions | 18 |
| **18** | Express one quantity as a percentage of another | 19 |
| **19** | Compare two quantities using percentages | 20 |
| **20** | Use standard units of mass, length, time, money | 21 |
| **21** | Round numbers to an appropriate degree of accuracy (dp); apply and interpret limits of accuracy | 22 |
| **22** | Round numbers to an appropriate degree of accuracy (sf); apply and interpret limits of accuracy | 23 |
| **23** | Estimate answers; check calculations using approximation and estimation | 24 |

**Algebra**

**24** Use algebraic notation — 25

**25** Interpret algebraic notation — 26

**26** Substitute numerical values into expressions — 27

**27** Substitute numerical values into scientific formulae and other formulae — 38

**28** Understand the difference between expressions, equations, inequalities, terms and factors — 29

**29** Simplify and manipulate algebraic expressions by collecting like terms — 30

**30** Simplify and manipulate algebraic expressions by multiplying a single term over a bracket — 31

**31** Simplify and manipulate algebraic expressions by taking out common factors — 32

**32** Simplify and manipulate algebraic expressions by expanding products of two binomials — 33

**33** Rearrange formulae to change the subject — 34

**34** Use algebraic methods to solve linear equations in one variable (part 1) — 35

**35** Use algebraic methods to solve linear equations in one variable (part 2) — 36

**36** Work with coordinates in all four quadrants — 37

**37** Recognise and sketch linear graphs — 38

**38** Recognise and sketch quadratic graphs — 39

**39** Interpret mathematical relationships algebraically — 40

**40** Interpret mathematical relationships graphically — 41

**41** Rearrange an equation into the form $y = mx + c$ — 42

**42** Use the form $y = mx + c$ to find gradients and intercepts — 43

**43** Use linear graphs to find approximate solutions to simultaneous linear equations — 44

**44** Generate terms of a sequence from a term-to-term rule — 45

**45** Generate terms of a sequence from a position-to-term rule — 46

**46** Recognise arithmetic sequences and find the $n$th term — 47

**47** Recognise geometric sequences and appreciate other sequences that arise — 48

**Ratio, proportion and rates of change**

**48** Change freely between related units (e.g. time, length, mass)  49

**49** Change freely between related compound units (e.g. area, volume/capacity)  50

**50** Use scale factors, scale diagrams and maps  51

**51** Express one quantity as a fraction of another  52

**52** Use ratio notation, including reduction to simplest form  53

**53** Divide a given quantity in a given ratio  54

**54** Express the division of a quantity into two parts as a ratio  55

**55** Express a multiplicative relationship between two quantities as a ratio or a fraction  56

**56** Solve problems involving percentage increase  57

**57** Solve problems involving percentage decrease  58

**58** Solve problems involving percentages by finding the original amount  59

**59** Solve problems involving simple interest  60

**60** Solve problems involving direct and inverse proportion  61

**61** Use compound units such as speed, unit pricing, and density  62

**Geometry and measures**

**62** Apply the formulae to calculate perimeter and area of triangles  63

**63** Apply the formulae to calculate perimeter and area of parallelograms  64

**64** Apply the formulae to calculate perimeter and area of trapezia  65

**65** Apply the properties of special types of quadrilaterals  66

**66** Apply the formula to calculate volume of cuboids  67

**67** Apply the formulae to calculate volume of prisms including cylinders  68

**68** Calculate: circumference of circles and perimeter of composite shapes  69

**69** Calculate: areas of circles and composite shapes  70

**70** Measure line segments and angles in geometric figures, including interpreting scale drawings  71

**71** Describe using conventional terms and notations: points, lines, parallel lines, Perpendicular lines, right angles, regular polygons, and other polygons that are reflectively and rotationally symmetric  72

**72** Use the standard convention for labelling triangles and use the basic congruence criteria for triangles (SSS, SAS, ASA, RHS)  73

**73** Identify and describe translations  75

**74** Identify and describe reflections  77

**75** Identify and describe rotations  78

**76** Apply the properties of angles at a point, angles at a point on a straight line, vertically opposite angles     79

**77** Understand and use alternate and corresponding angles on parallel lines     81

**78** Use the sum of angles in a triangle (e.g. to deduce and use the angle sum in any polygon)     83

**79** Use Pythagoras' Theorem     84

**80** Know the formulae for the trig ratios and apply them to find angles     85

**81** Know the formulae for the trig ratios and apply them to find lengths     86

**82** Interpret mathematical relationships both algebraically and geometrically     88

## Probability

**83** Analyse the frequency of outcomes of simple probability experiments involving randomness, fairness, equally and unequally likely outcomes, using appropriate language and the 0-1 probability scale     89

**84** Understand that the probabilities of all possible outcomes sum to 1     90

**85** Enumerate sets and unions/intersections of sets using tables     92

**86** Enumerate sets and unions/intersections of sets using grids     94

**87** Enumerate sets and unions/intersections of sets using Venn diagrams     95

**88** Construct theoretical possibility spaces for single and combined experiments with Equally likely, mutually exclusive outcomes and use these to calculate theoretical probabilities     96

## Statistics

**89** Construct tables, charts and diagrams     98

**90** Interpret tables, charts and diagrams     99

**91** Interpret appropriate graphical representation involving discrete, continuous and grouped data     101

**92** Calculate median, mean, mode and range     103

**93** Interpret scatter graphs of bivariate data; recognise correlation     104

**Answers**     106

**Record sheet**     123

# Introduction

*Collins Assessment Recall Tests for Maths* provides over 90 photocopiable tests covering the KS3 curriculum to help with long term memory for GCSE 9-1. As stand-alone tests, independent of any teaching and learning scheme, the 10-minute 1-page tests provide a structured way to assess core KS3 knowledge, to identify areas for development, and to provide evidence of progress.

## Retrieval practice

Retrieval practice is bringing something to mind that you have learnt before. When you put effort into retrieving information, you remember it better. Cognitive scientists have found that retrieval practice has the most powerful effect on long-term learning compared to other methods of studying.

## How to use this book

Regular recall of previously taught KS3 content will help your students to be secure in their core knowledge and to internalise it. You can use the 10-minute tests whenever you like and in any year, for example, Year 9, 10 and 11. You can repeat the tests at regular intervals to see if your students have improved. Students can record their attempts using the record sheet provided.

Each test has up to 10 questions, short answers and is worth 10 marks. The questions use command words from GCSE 9-1 and are organised into the Key Stage 3 Mathematics Programmes of Study six strands: Number; Algebra; Ratio, proportion and rates of change; Geometry and measures; Probability; and Statistics.

## Marking the tests

An easy-to-use mark scheme and answers is provided to show you how the marks are allocated.

## Recording progress

You can use the student record sheet to provide evidence of which areas your students have performed well in and where they need to focus. A spreadsheet is provided in the downloadable version so you can easily record results for your classes, and identify any gaps in understanding. The spreadsheet can then be used to inform your next teaching and learning steps.

## Editable download

All the files are available in Word and PDF format for you to edit if you wish. Go to collins.co.uk/assessment/downloads to find the instructions on how to download. The files are password protected and the password clue is included on the website. You will need to use the clue to locate the password in your book.

# Number 1: Understand and use place value for decimals, measures and integers of any size

**1** Write in figures, seven thousand and thirty-nine. [1 mark]

_____

**2** Write in figures, fifty-eight thousand and six. [1 mark]

_____

**3** Write in figures, seven and four tenths. [1 mark]

_____

**4** Write in figures, twenty and sixty-three thousandths. [1 mark]

_____

**5** Write the value of 3 in 56 309. [1 mark]

_____

**6** Write the value of 5 in 7.095 28. [1 mark]

_____

**7** Write the value of 4 in 47 805 kilometres. [1 mark]

_____

**8** Write the value of 2 in 0.004 209 millimetres. [1 mark]

_____

**9** Write the following in order from largest to smallest.

thirty-six hundredths, five tenths, seventy-four thousandths, eight hundredths [2 marks]

_____

**Total marks** _____ /10

# Number 2: Order positive integers, decimals and fractions

**1** Write the following integers in order, smallest first.                      **[1 mark]**

5, 10, 3, 0, 12, 13

_____

**2** Write the following decimals in order, smallest first.                      **[1 mark]**

3.4, 0.345, 0.345, 3.402, 3.411, 3.398

_____

**3** Write the following fractions in order, smallest first.                      **[1 mark]**

$\dfrac{7}{8}, \dfrac{1}{4}, \dfrac{3}{4}, \dfrac{1}{2}, \dfrac{2}{3}$

_____

**4** Write any fraction between $\dfrac{3}{8}$ and $\dfrac{1}{2}$.                      **[1 mark]**

_____

**5** Write any decimal between 0.71 and 0.72.                      **[1 mark]**

_____

**6** Write the following in order from largest to smallest.                      **[1 mark]**

$6\dfrac{1}{4}, 2\dfrac{1}{2}, 6\dfrac{1}{8}, 2\dfrac{3}{4}, \dfrac{4}{7}$

_____

**7** Write the following in order from largest to smallest.                      **[2 marks]**

$2.41, 2\dfrac{1}{3}, 2\dfrac{2}{5}, 2\dfrac{9}{20}, 2.333$

_____

**8** Write down the greatest 4-digit number and the least 4-digit number that starts with 5 and
ends in 1.                      **[2 marks]**

_____    _____

**Total marks _____ /10**

# Number 3: Order negative integers, decimals and fractions

**1** Write the following integers in order, smallest first. [1 mark]

4, −11, 2, −1, 0, −13

_____

**2** Write the following decimals in order, smallest first. [1 mark]

−2.3, −0.236, −2.304, −2.29, −2.374

_____

**3** Write the following fractions in order, smallest first. [1 mark]

$-\dfrac{4}{5}, -\dfrac{1}{3}, -\dfrac{3}{4}, -\dfrac{1}{2}, -\dfrac{1}{4}$

_____

**4** Write any fraction between $-\dfrac{4}{5}$ and $-\dfrac{1}{2}$ . [1 mark]

_____

**5** Write any decimal between −0.1 and 0. [1 mark]

_____

**6** Write the following in order from largest to smallest. [1 mark]

$3\dfrac{1}{4}, -1\dfrac{1}{2}, 3\dfrac{1}{8}, -1\dfrac{3}{4}, \dfrac{3}{2}$

_____

**7** Write the following in order from largest to smallest. [2 marks]

$-5.62, -5\dfrac{2}{3}, -5\dfrac{2}{5}, -5\dfrac{17}{20}, -5.666$

_____

**8** Write down the greatest 4-digit negative integer and the least 4-digit negative integer that starts and ends with either a 3 or a 4. [2 marks]

_____  _____

Total marks _____ /10

# Number 4: Use the symbols =, ≠, <, >, ≤, ≥

**1** Write the correct symbol from this list =, ≠, <, >, ≤, ≥ into the box. **[1 mark]**

5 ☐ 7

**2** Write the correct symbol from this list =, ≠, <, >, ≤, ≥ into the box. **[1 mark]**

−4 ☐ −3.6

**3** Write the correct symbol from this list =, ≠, <, >, ≤, ≥ into the box. **[1 mark]**

0.7 ☐ $\frac{7}{10}$

**4** Write the correct symbol from this list =, ≠, <, >, ≤, ≥ into the box. **[1 mark]**

7 − 5 ☐ 5 − 7

**5** Write the correct symbol from this list =, ≠, <, >, ≤, ≥ into the box. **[1 mark]**

$6\frac{1}{3}$ ☐ 6.333

**6** Write the correct symbol from this list =, ≠, <, >, ≤, ≥ into the box. **[1 mark]**

$2\frac{1}{4}$ ☐ −2.25

**7** Write down all the positive integers ≤5. **[2 marks]**

_____

**8** Write down all the negative integers >−4. **[2 marks]**

_____

**Total marks _____ /10**

# Number 5: Work with prime numbers and express a number as the product of prime factors

1  Work out which of the following are prime numbers.                    [1 mark]

   1, 2, 5, 9, 11, 15, 19

   _____

2  Work out which of the following numbers are divisible by 3.          [1 mark]

   3, 13, 23, 33, 39, 51, 59

   _____

3  Write the remainder when these numbers are divided by 5.             [1 mark]

   78, 5551

   _____

4  Write down a prime number in the 90s.                                [1 mark]

   _____

5  Write 132 as the product of prime factors.                          [1 mark]

   _____

6  Write 135 as the product of prime factors.                          [1 mark]

   _____

7  Write 360 as the product of prime factors.                          [2 marks]

   _____

8  Write down the 12$^{th}$ and the 21$^{st}$ prime numbers.           [2 marks]

   _____  _____

                                        Total marks _____ /10

# Number 6: Work out HCF (highest common factor) of two or more numbers using any method

1 Work out the highest common factor of 12 and 18. **[1 mark]**

_____

2 Work out the highest common factor of 20 and 40. **[1 mark]**

_____

3 Work out the highest common factor of 30 and 45. **[1 mark]**

_____

4 Work out the highest common factor of 90 and 132. **[1 mark]**

_____

5 Work out the highest common factor of 8, 12 and 20. **[1 mark]**

_____

6 Work out the highest common factor of 84, 126, and 210. **[1 mark]**

_____

7 The highest common factor of two numbers is 12.
One of the numbers is 24. Work out the smallest possible value of the other number. **[2 marks]**

_____

8 The highest common factor of three numbers is 30.
Two of the numbers are 90 and 150. The other number has a factor of 7.
Work out the smallest possible value of the other number. **[2 marks]**

_____

**Total marks** _____ **/10**

# Number 7: Work out LCM (lowest common multiple) of two or more numbers using any method

No calculator

**1** Work out the lowest common multiple of 3 and 5.  **[1 mark]**

_____

**2** Work out the lowest common multiple of 10 and 7.  **[1 mark]**

_____

**3** Work out the lowest common multiple of 12 and 30.  **[1 mark]**

_____

**4** Work out the lowest common multiple of 70 and 60.  **[1 mark]**

_____

**5** Work out lowest common multiple of 6, 12 and 20.  **[1 mark]**

_____

**6** Work out the lowest common multiple of 18, 20, and 75.  **[1 mark]**

_____

**7** The lowest common multiple of two numbers is 150.
One of the numbers is 25. Work out the smallest possible value of the other number.  **[2 marks]**

_____

**8** The lowest common multiple of three numbers is 360.
Two of the numbers are 20 and 90. The other number has a factor of 7.
Work out the smallest possible value of the other number.  **[2 marks]**

_____

**Total marks _____ /10**

# Number 8: Apply the four operations to integers, both positive and negative

**1** Work out $(-5) + (-3)$. **[1 mark]**

_____

**2** Work out $(-4) - (-10)$. **[1 mark]**

_____

**3** Work out $(+3) \times (-5)$. **[1 mark]**

_____

**4** Work out $(-20) \div (-5)$. **[1 mark]**

_____

**5** Work out $(-16) + 4 + (-8)$. **[1 mark]**

_____

**6** Work out $-3 - -4 + -5$. **[1 mark]**

_____

**7** Work out $-3 + 4 \times -4$. **[2 marks]**

_____

**8** Work out $-12 \div -2 + 6$. **[2 marks]**

_____

**Total marks _____ /10**

# Number 9: Apply the four operations to decimals, both positive and negative

**1** Work out 60.39 + 5.81.

[1 mark]

_____

**2** Work out 6.3 – 0.87.

[1 mark]

_____

**3** Work out 0.7 × 0.5.

[1 mark]

_____

**4** Work out 6.3 ÷ 0.09.

[1 mark]

_____

**5** Work out –1.6 × 0.55.

[1 mark]

_____

**6** Work out –3 ÷ 0.06.

[1 mark]

_____

**7** Work out 0.010 3 × 2.6.

[2 marks]

_____

**8** Work out –0.358 8 ÷ –0.023.

[2 marks]

_____

**Total marks _____ /10**

## Number 10: Apply + and – to simple fractions, (including improper fractions and mixed numbers) both positive and negative

No calculator

**1** Work out $\frac{1}{3} + \frac{2}{5}$. [1 mark]

_____

**2** Work out $\frac{3}{4} - \frac{1}{7}$. [1 mark]

_____

**3** Work out $\frac{2}{3} - \frac{3}{4}$. [1 mark]

_____

**4** Work out $1\frac{1}{2} + 2\frac{1}{8}$. [1 mark]

_____

**5** Work out $3\frac{2}{5} - 1\frac{7}{10}$. [1 mark]

_____

**6** Work out $2\frac{3}{7} + 1\frac{1}{5} - \frac{7}{10}$. [1 mark]

_____

**7** Work out $\frac{1}{3} - \frac{7}{12} + \frac{5}{4}$. [2 marks]

_____

**8** Work out $\left(1\frac{1}{2} + 3\frac{1}{4}\right) - \left(2\frac{2}{5} - 4\frac{1}{3}\right)$. [2 marks]

_____

Total marks _____ /10

## Number 11: Apply × and ÷ to simple fractions, (including improper fractions and mixed numbers) both positive and negative

No calculator

**1** Work out $\frac{1}{3} \times \frac{2}{5}$.

[1 mark]

_____

**2** Work out $\frac{3}{4} \div \frac{1}{7}$.

[1 mark]

_____

**3** Work out $\frac{3}{8} \times \frac{2}{9}$.

[1 mark]

_____

**4** Work out $\frac{6}{7} \div \frac{3}{28}$.

[1 mark]

_____

**5** Work out $2\frac{1}{5} \times -\frac{10}{11}$.

[1 mark]

_____

**6** Work out $-3\frac{1}{8} \div -1\frac{1}{4}$.

[1 mark]

_____

**7** Work out $2\frac{1}{4} \times \frac{3}{8} \div \frac{5}{9}$.

[2 marks]

_____

**8** Work out $\left(3\frac{1}{2} \div -2\frac{2}{5}\right) \times -\frac{9}{10}$.

[2 marks]

_____

**Total marks** _____ /10

# Number 12: Use conventional notation for priority of operations, including brackets, powers, roots and reciprocals

**1** Work out $3 + 4 \times 5$. **[1 mark]**

_____

**2** Work out $12 \div 3 - 5$. **[1 mark]**

_____

**3** What is the reciprocal of $\frac{2}{5}$? **[1 mark]**

_____

**4** Work out $(5 + 5 \times 5) \div 5$. **[1 mark]**

_____

**5** Write brackets in this calculation to make it true. **[1 mark]**

$4 + 3^2 = 49$

_____

**6** Work out $\sqrt{98 + 1 \times 2}$. **[1 mark]**

_____

**7** Write brackets in this calculation to make it true. **[1 mark]**

$\sqrt{55 - 5} \div 2$

_____

**8** Write brackets in this calculation to make it true. **[1 mark]**

$1 + 3^2 - 8 + 2 = 0$

_____

**9** Work out the reciprocal of $4 \times 5^2 \div \sqrt{100}$. **[2 marks]**

_____

Total marks _____ /10

## Number 13: Use positive integer powers and associated real roots (square, cube and higher)

No calculator

**1** Work out the value of $3^4$.

[1 mark]

_____

**2** Work out the value of $2^5$.

[1 mark]

_____

**3** Work out the value of $10^5$.

[1 mark]

_____

**4** Work out the value of $7^3$.

[1 mark]

_____

**5** Work out the value of $\sqrt[3]{1000}$.

[1 mark]

_____

**6** Work out the value of $\sqrt[4]{81}$.

[1 mark]

_____

**7** Work out the value of $25^5 \sqrt{25}$.

[2 marks]

_____

**8** Work out the value of $(2^2 + 3^3) \div \sqrt{100}$.

[2 marks]

_____

Total marks _____ /10

# Number 14: Recognise powers of 2, 3, 4, 5

`No calculator`

**1** Write 8 as a power of 2. **[1 mark]**

_____

**2** Write 9 as a power of 3. **[1 mark]**

_____

**3** Write 64 as a power of 4. **[1 mark]**

_____

**4** Write 81 as a power of 3. **[1 mark]**

_____

**5** Write 625 as a power of 5. **[1 mark]**

_____

**6** Write 512 as a power of 2. **[1 mark]**

_____

**7** Show that $5^3 + 3 = 2^7$. **[2 marks]**

_____

_____

**8** Show that $2^3 \times 5^3 + 24 = 2^{10}$. **[2 marks]**

_____

_____

**Total marks _____ /10**

# Number 15: Distinguish between exact representations of roots and their decimal approximations

`No calculator`

**1** Write down which of the following numbers has an exact square root. **[1 mark]**

12, 24, 36, 48, 60, 72, 84

_____

**2** Write down which of the following numbers has an exact cube root. **[1 mark]**

4, 8, 12, 16, 20, 24

_____

**3** Write down the two positive consecutive integers between which $\sqrt{70}$ lies. **[1 mark]**

_____

**4** Write down the two positive consecutive integers between which $\sqrt{890}$ lies. **[1 mark]**

_____

**5** Explain why this statement is false: $\sqrt{2} = 1.414$. **[1 mark]**

_____

**6** Explain why this statement is false: $\sqrt{0.64} = 0.08$ **[1 mark]**

_____

**7** Show that this statement is true: $\dfrac{\sqrt{25}}{\sqrt[3]{1000}} = 0.5$ **[2 marks]**

_____

**8** Give two numbers greater than 0 and less than 1 that have an exact cube root. **[2 marks]**

_____

Total marks _____ /10

# Number 16: Interpret and compare numbers in standard form $A \times 10^n$ (where $n$ is an integer)

1  Write 3700 in standard form. **[1 mark]**

_____

2  Write 0.046 in standard form. **[1 mark]**

_____

3  Write 5 in standard form. **[1 mark]**

_____

4  Write $4.7 \times 10^2$ as an ordinary number. **[1 mark]**

_____

5  Write $6.2 \times 10^{-3}$ as a decimal number. **[1 mark]**

_____

6  Write $4.56 \times 10^0$ as a decimal number. **[1 mark]**

_____

7  Write the largest of these numbers as an ordinary number. **[2 marks]**

$9.8 \times 10^{-3}$, $8.2 \times 10^{-5}$, $3.1 \times 10^1$

_____

8  Write the smallest of these numbers as a decimal number. **[2 marks]**

$1.04 \times 10^3$, $2.1 \times 10^{-4}$, $3.17 \times 10^0$, $5.4 \times 10^{-1}$

_____

**Total marks _____ /10**

# Number 17: Work interchangeably with terminating decimals and their corresponding fractions

No calculator

**1** Write $\frac{1}{4}$ as a decimal.

[1 mark]

_____

**2** Write $\frac{4}{5}$ as a decimal.

[1 mark]

_____

**3** Write $3\frac{7}{8}$ as a decimal.

[1 mark]

_____

**4** Write 0.4 as a fraction in its simplest form.

[1 mark]

_____

**5** Write 0.15 as a fraction in its simplest form.

[1 mark]

_____

**6** Write 8.125 as a mixed number in its simplest form.

[1 mark]

_____

**7** Write the following in order of size, smallest first.

[2 marks]

$\frac{37}{10}, 3\frac{4}{7}, 3\frac{3}{4}, \frac{7}{2}, 3.4$

_____

**8** Write the following in order of size, largest first.

[2 marks]

$5\frac{1}{2}, \frac{45}{8}, 5.3, \frac{21}{4}, \frac{58}{10}$

_____

Total marks _____ /10

# Number 18: Express one quantity as a percentage of another

1 Write 5 kg as a percentage of 20 kg. **[1 mark]**

_____

2 Write £40 as a percentage of £80. **[1 mark]**

_____

3 Write 60 cm as a percentage of 30 cm. **[1 mark]**

_____

4 Write 36 cm$^2$ as a percentage of 48 cm$^2$. **[1 mark]**

_____

5 Write 10p as a percentage of £1. **[1 mark]**

_____

6 Write 2.16 m as a percentage of 2 m. **[1 mark]**

_____

7 Write 69 g as a percentage of 84 g. **[2 marks]**

_____

8 Write 0.42 km as a percentage of 98 km. **[2 marks]**

_____

Total marks _____ /10

# Number 19: Compare two quantities using percentages

**1** Use percentages to work out the better mark:    **[2 marks]**

41 out of 60 or 11 out of 15.

_____

**2** Work out the higher percentage of sugar:    **[2 marks]**

51 g of sugar in 80 g of biscuit or 78 g of sugar in 132 g of biscuit.

_____

**3** Work out the lower percentage of salt:    **[2 marks]**

0.2 g of salt in 150 g of cereal or 0.17 g of salt in 123 g of cereal.

_____

**4** Work out the better percentage wage increase:    **[2 marks]**

£130 on £21 200 or £145 on £23 500.

_____

**5** Work out the better percentage loss:    **[2 marks]**

6.4 kg off 88.3 kg or 2.9 kg off 42.6 kg.

_____

**Total marks _____ /10**

# Number 20: Use standard units of mass, length, time, money

1   Write these units of mass in order of size, smallest first.                    **[1 mark]**

    tonne, gram, kilogram

    _____

2   Write these units of mass in order of size, largest first.                     **[1 mark]**

    centimetre, metre, millimetre, kilometre

    _____

3   Write these units of time in order of size, smallest first.                    **[1 mark]**

    week, second, day, hour, year, minute, month

    _____

4   A train leaves a station at 07:35. It takes 1 hour 28 minutes to arrive at the next station.
    Work out the time that the train arrives.                                      **[1 mark]**

    _____

5   Work out the cost of three books, each costing £5.99.                          **[1 mark]**

    _____

6   Write down what you think is the height of your teacher in centimetres.         **[1 mark]**

    _____

7   Three lengths of string, 43 cm, 72 cm and 29 cm are cut from a piece 2 m long.
    Work out the length that remains.                                              **[2 marks]**

    _____

8   Three bags of sweets, 125 g, 220 g and 1 kg are taken from a box containing 2 kg of sweets.
    Work out the mass that remains.                                                **[2 marks]**

    _____

                                                          **Total marks _____ /10**

# Number 21: Round numbers to an appropriate degree of accuracy (dp); apply and interpret limits of accuracy

**1** Write 3.412 to 2 decimal places.

[1 mark]

_____

**2** Write 0.069 857 to 3 decimal places.

[1 mark]

_____

**3** Write 5.549 to 1 decimal place.

[1 mark]

_____

**4** Calculate $2.357 \div 7$ and write the answer to 3 decimal places.

[1 mark]

_____

**5** Calculate $0.062 \times 0.377$ and write the answer to 4 decimal places.

[1 mark]

_____

**6** Calculate $3.718 + 4.3 \times 1.62$ and write the answer to 2 decimal places.

[1 mark]

_____

**7** The width of a door is measured as 1.47 m to 2 decimal places.
Write down the minimum and maximum lengths it could be.

[2 marks]

_____ _____

**8** A rectangle measures 6.4 cm by 5.3 cm, each measurement is to 1 decimal place.
Calculate its minimum area.

[2 marks]

_____

Total marks _____ /10

# Number 22: Round numbers to an appropriate degree of accuracy (sf); apply and interpret limits of accuracy

1  Write 41.843 to 2 significant figures. [1 mark]

_____

2  Write 0.078 12 to 3 significant figures. [1 mark]

_____

3  Write 579 832 to 1 significant figure. [1 mark]

_____

4  Calculate 0.032 8 × 7 and write the answer to 3 significant figures. [1 mark]

_____

5  Calculate 0.189 ÷ 0.003 7 and write the answer to 4 significant figures. [1 mark]

_____

6  Calculate 2100 − 781 × 0.4 and write the answer to 2 significant figures. [1 mark]

_____

7  The mass of a teacher is 81.0 kg to 3 significant figures.
Write down the minimum and maximum possible mass of the teacher. [2 marks]

_____  _____

8  Sandra sends 9 tweets of 140 characters every day one leap year.
Calculate the total number of characters. Give your answer to 3 significant figures. [2 marks]

_____

Total marks _____ /10

# Number 23: Estimate answers; check calculations using approximation and estimation

`No calculator`

**1** Estimate the value of 6.2 × 4.81. [1 mark]

_____

**2** Estimate the value of 104 ÷ 9.81. [1 mark]

_____

**3** Estimate the value of $\sqrt{391}$. [1 mark]

_____

**4** Estimate the value of $47.5^2$. [1 mark]

_____

**5** Estimate the value of $0.0321^2$. [1 mark]

_____

**6** Estimate the value of $\sqrt{0.981}$. [1 mark]

_____

**7** Peta says $\dfrac{3.4 \times 5.68}{0.298}$ is 6.48 to 3 significant figures. [2 marks]

Estimate the answer and state whether he could be correct.

_____

**8** Aisha says $\dfrac{7910}{\sqrt{104} \times 0.84}$ is 923 to 3 significant figures. [2 marks]

Estimate the answer and state whether she could be correct.

_____

**Total marks** _____ /10

# Algebra 24: Use algebraic notation

**1** Simplify $p \times q$. [1 mark]

_____

**2** Simplify $e + e + e + e$. [1 mark]

_____

**3** Simplify $g \times 7$. [1 mark]

_____

**4** Simplify $n \times n \times n$. [1 mark]

_____

**5** Simplify $c \times c \times d$. [1 mark]

_____

**6** Simplify $(m + m + m) \div 5$. [1 mark]

_____

**7** Simplify for $h \div 0.5 + h$. [2 marks]

_____

**8** Simplify $(6 \times a - c - c - c - c - c) \times 7$ [2 marks]

_____

Total marks _____ /10

# Algebra 25: Interpret algebraic notation

**1** On Monday, Rob sends $m$ tweets and Jay sends $n$ tweets. **[1 mark]**

Write an expression for the total number of tweets they send.

_____

**2** Amina writes a story containing $r$ words. Javid writes a story containing 60 words fewer. **[1 mark]**

Write an expression for the number of words in Javid's story.

_____

**3** Julia has lived for a total of $s$ days. Chris is older than Julia and has lived for $t$ days. **[1 mark]**

Write an expression for the number of days Chris is older than Julia.

_____

**4** Each floor in a multi-story car park is 3.5 metres high. **[1 mark]**

Write an expression for the total height of a multi-story car park that has $y$ floors and a roof that is 0.5 metres thick.

_____

**5** An egg costs $x$ pence. Write an expression for the cost of six eggs in pence. **[2 marks]**

Now write an expression for the cost of 10 eggs in pounds.

_____   _____

**6** There are $p$ grams of flour in a bag. It is shared equally between 8 cakes. **[2 marks]**

Write down an expression for the amount of flour in grams in each cake.

Now write an expression for the amount of flour in kilograms in 800 cakes.

_____   _____

**7** A scientist counts $n$ bacteria in a dish. The number of bacteria doubles every day. **[2 marks]**

Write an expression for the number of bacteria in the dish 3 days later.

Write an expression for the number of bacteria in the dish $t$ days later.

_____   _____

**Total marks** _____ /10

# Algebra 26: Substitute numerical values into expressions

**1** Work out the value of $3a + 4b$ when $a = 3$ and $b = 2$. [1 mark]

_____

**2** Work out the value of $5m - 3n$ when $m = 5$ and $n = 4$. [1 mark]

_____

**3** Work out the value of $c^2 - 5d$ when $c = 4$ and $d = 1$. [1 mark]

_____

**4** Work out the value of $2p^3 - 3$ when $p = 3$. [1 mark]

_____

**5** Work out the value of $\dfrac{e}{5} - f^2$ when $e = 10$ and $f = -2$. [1 mark]

_____

**6** Work out the value of $\dfrac{1}{2}r^2 + 3r$ when $r = 6$. [1 mark]

_____

**7** Work out the value of $3(4 - s) + 2(t^2 + 3)$ when $s = 5$ and $t = 3$. [2 marks]

_____

**8** Work out the value of $\dfrac{5(u + 7)}{3v - 6}$ when $u = -1$ and $v = 5$. [2 marks]

_____

**Total marks _____ /10**

# Algebra 27: Substitute numerical values into scientific formulae and other formulae

**1** Calculate the value of $V$ to 1 decimal place in the formula $V = IR$ if $I = 5.3$ and $R = 4.7$. **[1 mark]**

_____

**2** Calculate the value of $R$ to 2 decimal places in the formula $R = \dfrac{V}{I}$ if $V = 4.5$ and $I = 6.3$. **[1 mark]**

_____

**3** Calculate the value of $C$ to 1 decimal place in the formula $C = 2\pi r$ if $r = 7.3$. **[1 mark]**

_____

**4** Calculate the value of $A$ to 2 decimal places in the formula $A = \pi r^2$ if $r = 4.1$. **[1 mark]**

_____

**5** Calculate the value of $C$ in the formula $C = \dfrac{5}{9}(F - 32)$ if $F = 140$. **[1 mark]**

_____

**6** Calculate the value of $F$ in the formula $F = \dfrac{9}{5}C + 32$ if $C = 25$. **[1 mark]**

_____

**7** Calculate the value of $s$ to 1 decimal place in the formula $s = \left(\dfrac{u + v}{2}\right)t$, **[2 marks]**

if $u = 5.7$, $v = 8.4$ and $t = 3.6$.

_____

**8** Calculate the value of $s$ to 2 significant figures in the formula $s = ut + \dfrac{1}{2}at^2$,

if $u = 8.2$, $a = 9.8$ and $t = 0.7$. **[2 marks]**

_____

Total marks _____ /10

## Algebra 28: Understand the difference between expressions, equations, inequalities, terms and factors

No calculator

1  Write down which of the following are expressions. **[1 mark]**

$y = 4x + 2$, $3x^2y$, $V = \dfrac{4}{3}\pi r^3$, $5m - 4n > 6p$, $4x + 6.4cd$, $4x \le 6y - 9$

_____

2  Write down which of the following are equations. **[1 mark]**

$y = 4x + 2$, $3x^2y$, $V = \dfrac{4}{3}\pi r^3$, $5m - 4n > 6p$, $4x + 6.4cd$, $4x \le 6y - 9$

_____

3  Write down which of the following are inequalities. **[1 mark]**

$y = 4x + 2$, $3x^2y$, $V = \dfrac{4}{3}\pi r^3$, $5m - 4n > 6p$, $4x + 6.4cd$, $4x \le 6y - 9$

_____

4  Write down the second term of this expression. **[1 mark]**

$2a - 3bc + 2d^2 - 5e$

_____

5  Write down a factor of this expression, other than 1. **[1 mark]**

$2x^2 - 6xy$

_____

6  Write down all the common factors of this expression, other than 1. **[1 mark]**

$5mn - 40n^2$

_____

7  Write down any two-term expression that has a common factor of $3x$. **[2 marks]**

_____

8  Explain the difference between an expression and an equation, giving an example of each that contains a term of $3x$. **[2 marks]**

_____

Total marks _____ /10

# Algebra 29: Simplify and manipulate algebraic expressions by collecting like terms

No calculator

**1** Simplify $a + 5a - 2a$.

[1 mark]

_____

**2** Simplify $2c + 4c - c$.

[1 mark]

_____

**3** Simplify $5x + 7y - 3y - 2x$.

[1 mark]

_____

**4** Simplify $3y + 8 - 4y$.

[1 mark]

_____

**5** Simplify $11w - 4 - 3w + 9$.

[1 mark]

_____

**6** Simplify $6e + 8f - 5e - 4f$.

[1 mark]

_____

**7** The expression $3x + 7y + ax + 5y$ simplifies to $9x + by$.

[2 marks]

Work out the values of $a$ and $b$.

_____

**8** The expression $cx + dy - 4y - 6x$ simplifies to $8x - y$.

[2 marks]

Work out the values of $c$ and $d$.

_____

**Total marks _____ /10**

# Algebra 30: Simplify and manipulate algebraic expressions by multiplying a single term over a bracket

**1** Expand $3(a + 2b)$. [1 mark]

_____

**2** Expand $x(2x - 1)$. [1 mark]

_____

**3** Expand $2b(3b + 4c)$. [1 mark]

_____

**4** Expand $4c(2 - 3c)$. [1 mark]

_____

**5** Expand and simplify $2g(g - 3) + 5g$. [1 mark]

_____

**6** Expand and simplify $7h - h(3h - 4)$. [1 mark]

_____

**7** Expand and simplify $2d(3d - 4) + 5(d - 3)$. [2 marks]

_____

**8** Expand and simplify $4e(5f - e) - 2f(3e - f)$. [2 marks]

_____

**Total marks** _____ /10

# Algebra 31: Simplify and manipulate algebraic expressions by taking out common factors

**1** Factorise $4a + 10$.

[1 mark]

_____

**2** Factorise $15 - 20b$.

[1 mark]

_____

**3** Factorise $6c^2 + 5c$.

[1 mark]

_____

**4** Factorise $14d - 18d^2$.

[1 mark]

_____

**5** Factorise $3e + 9e^2$.

[1 mark]

_____

**6** Factorise $f^3 - 4f^2$.

[1 mark]

_____

**7** Factorise $6g + 9g^2 + 21g^3$.

[2 marks]

_____

**8** Factorise $16m^2n^2 - 2m^3n + 4mn^3$.

[2 marks]

_____

**Total marks** _____ /10

# Algebra 32: Simplify and manipulate algebraic expressions by expanding products of two binomials

**1** Expand and simplify $(a + 3)(a + 2)$. [1 mark]

_____

**2** Expand and simplify $(b + 3)(b - 4)$. [1 mark]

_____

**3** Expand and simplify $(c - 5)(c + 6)$. [1 mark]

_____

**4** Expand and simplify $(d - 3)(d - 7)$. [1 mark]

_____

**5** Expand and simplify $(2e + 1)(3e + 2)$. [1 mark]

_____

**6** Expand and simplify $(4 + 3f)(2 - f)$. [1 mark]

_____

**7** Expand and simplify $(2g - 3)(3g - 2)$. [2 marks]

_____

**8** Expand and simplify $(3h - 4)(5 - 2h)$. [2 marks]

_____

**Total marks** _____ /10

# Algebra 33: Rearrange formulae to change the subject

**1** Make $d$ the subject of the formula $C = \pi d$. [1 mark]

_____

**2** Make $r$ the subject of the formula $A = \pi r^2$. [1 mark]

_____

**3** Make $u$ the subject of the formula $v = u + at$. [1 mark]

_____

**4** Make $a$ the subject of the formula $v = u + at$. [1 mark]

_____

**5** Make $u$ the subject of the formula $v^2 = u^2 + {}^2as$. [1 mark]

_____

**6** Make $F$ the subject of the formula $C = \dfrac{5}{9}(F - 32)$. [1 mark]

_____

**7** Make $v$ the subject of the formula $s = \left(\dfrac{u + v}{2}\right)t$. [2 marks]

_____

**8** Make $f$ the subject of the formula $\dfrac{1}{u} + \dfrac{1}{v} = \dfrac{1}{f}$. [2 marks]

_____

Total marks _____ /10

# Algebra 34: Use algebraic methods to solve linear equations in one variable (part 1)

No calculator

**1** Solve $a + 7 = 11$.

[1 mark]

_____

**2** Solve $15 = 5b$.

[1 mark]

_____

**3** Solve $6 + 2c = 9$.

[1 mark]

_____

**4** Solve $11 = 7 - 3d$.

[1 mark]

_____

**5** Solve $5(e + 2) = 40$.

[1 mark]

_____

**6** Solve $21 = 3(2f - 7)$.

[1 mark]

_____

**7** Solve $8 - 2(3g + 2) = 0$.

[2 marks]

_____

**8** Solve $16 = 4 - 3(6 - 5g)$.

[2 marks]

_____

**Total marks** _____ /10

# Algebra 35: Use algebraic methods to solve linear equations in one variable (part 2)

No calculator

1  Solve $3j = 6 + 2j$

[1 mark]

_____

2  Solve $5 - 2k = 4k$.

[1 mark]

_____

3  Solve $7 + 3m = 5m - 3$.

[1 mark]

_____

4  Solve $4 + n = 3(n - 7)$.

[1 mark]

_____

5  Solve $2(3 - 2p) = 8$.

[1 mark]

_____

6  Solve $11 = 5 - 2(2q - 1)$.

[1 mark]

_____

7  Solve $2(6 + 5r) = 3(2r + 1) + 4$.

[2 marks]

_____

8  Solve $7 - 2(3 - 2s) = 5(2s + 1) - 8$.

[2 marks]

_____

Total marks _____ /10

# Algebra 36: Work with coordinates in all four quadrants

`No calculator`

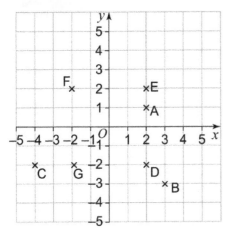

**1** Write down the coordinates of A.                                                                 **[1 mark]**

_____

**2** Write down the coordinates of B.                                                                 **[1 mark]**

_____

**3** Write down the coordinates of C.                                                                 **[1 mark]**

_____

**4** Write down the coordinates of the origin.                                                        **[1 mark]**

_____

**5** Write down the letter at the point with coordinates (–2, 2).                                      **[1 mark]**

_____

**6** Write down the coordinates of the point that is half-way between points E and F.                  **[1 mark]**

_____

**7** Write down the coordinates of the point that is half-way between points A and D.                  **[2 marks]**

_____

**8** Write down the coordinates of the point that is half-way between points B and F.                  **[2 marks]**

_____

Total marks _____ /10

# Algebra 37: Recognise and sketch linear graphs

No calculator. Graph paper required.

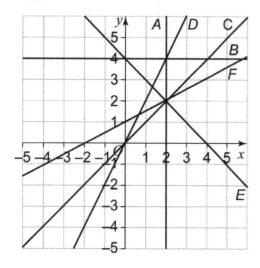

1  Write down the equation of line A.                                                           **[1 mark]**

_____

2  Write down the equation of line B.                                                           **[1 mark]**

_____

3  Write down the equation of line C.                                                           **[1 mark]**

_____

4  Write down the equation of line D.                                                           **[1 mark]**

_____

5  Write down the equation of line E.                                                           **[1 mark]**

_____

6  Write down the equation of line F.                                                           **[1 mark]**

_____

7  Sketch the graph with equation $y = 3 + 2x$ on separate graph paper.                         **[2 marks]**

8  Sketch the graph with equation $y = 6 - x$ on separate graph paper.                           **[2 marks]**


Total marks _____ /10

# Algebra 38: Recognise and sketch quadratic graphs

No calculator. Graph paper required.

**1** Which of these equations does NOT give a quadratic graph? **[1 mark]**

    **A** $y = 3x^2$         **B** $y + 3x = 2 - x^2$         **C** $y = x^2 + x^3 - 2$         **D** $x^2 = y + 4$

_____

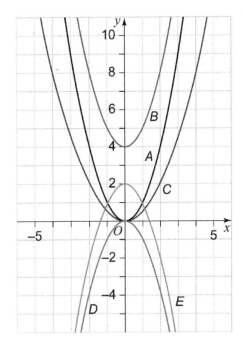

**2** Write down the equation of graph A. **[1 mark]**

_____

**3** Write down the equation of graph B. **[1 mark]**

_____

**4** Write down the equation of graph C. **[1 mark]**

_____

**5** Write down the equation of graph D. **[1 mark]**

_____

**6** Write down the equation of graph E. **[1 mark]**

_____

**7** Sketch the graph with equation $y = 2 + x^2$ on separate graph paper. **[2 marks]**

**8** Sketch the graph with equation $y = 5 - x^2$ on separate graph paper. **[2 marks]**

Total marks _____ /10

# Algebra 39: Interpret mathematical relationships algebraically

**1** $a$ is 3 more than $b$. **[1 mark]**

Write this relationship as an equation.

_____

**2** $c$ is twice the value of $d$. **[1 mark]**

Write this relationship as an equation.

_____

**3** $e$ is 5 less than $f$. **[1 mark]**

Write this relationship as an equation.

_____

**4** $g$ is one quarter of $h$. **[1 mark]**

Write this relationship as an equation.

_____

**5** $j$ multiplied by 5 is equal to 2 more than $k$. **[1 mark]**

Write this relationship as an equation.

_____

**6** $m$ divided by $n$ is equal to $p$. **[1 mark]**

Write this relationship as an equation.

_____

**7** 6 less than half of $q$ is equal to 5 less than $r$. **[2 marks]**

Write this relationship as an equation.

_____

**8** The product of $t$ and 7 is 2 more than the reciprocal of $b$. **[2 marks]**

Write this relationship as an equation.

_____

**Total marks _____ /10**

# Algebra 40: Interpret mathematical relationships graphically

**1** The value of $x$ is 3 for all values of $y$. [1 mark]

Sketch the graph of this relationship.

**2** The value of $y$ is $-1$ for all values of $x$. [1 mark]

Sketch the graph of this relationship.

**3** The value of $y$ is twice the value of $x$. [1 mark]

Sketch the graph of this relationship.

**4** The value of $x$ is one-third the value of $y$. [1 mark]

Sketch the graph of this relationship.

**5** The value of $y$ is three more than the value of $x$. [1 mark]

Sketch the graph of this relationship.

**6** The value of $y$ divided by $x$ is 1. [1 mark]

Sketch the graph of this relationship.

**7** The value of $y$ is equal to the value of the square of $x$. [2 marks]

Sketch the graph of this relationship.

**8** The value of $x$ squared is two less than the value of $y$. [2 marks]

Sketch the graph of this relationship.

Total marks _____ /10

## Algebra 41: Rearrange an equation into the form $y = mx + c$

No calculator

**1** Rearrange $2y = 6x + 4$ into the form $y = mx + c$. **[1 mark]**

_____

**2** Rearrange $\frac{1}{2}y = 3x - 5$ into the form $y = mx + c$. **[1 mark]**

_____

**3** Rearrange $2y - 4 = x$ into the form $y = mx + c$. **[1 mark]**

_____

**4** Rearrange $4y + 3 = 5x$ into the form $y = mx + c$. **[1 mark]**

_____

**5** Rearrange $x + \frac{1}{4}y = 5$ into the form $y = mx + c$. **[1 mark]**

_____

**6** Rearrange $3x + 4y + 12 = 0$ into the form $y = mx + c$. **[1 mark]**

_____

**7** Rearrange $\frac{1}{5}y - 2x + 3 = 0$ into the form $y = mx + c$. **[2 marks]**

_____

**8** Rearrange $2\left(\frac{3}{2}y - 4\right) + 5x = 7$ into the form $y = mx + c$. **[2 marks]**

_____

**Total marks** _____ /10

# Algebra 42: Use the form $y = mx + c$ to find gradients and intercepts

**1** Work out the gradient and intercepts on the $y$-axis and $x$-axis
of the line $3y = 4x - 5$.  **[2 marks]**

_____

_____

**2** Work out the gradient and intercepts on the $y$-axis and $x$-axis
of the line $2x + 3y + 4 = 0$.  **[2 marks]**

_____

_____

**3** Work out the gradient and intercepts on the $y$-axis and $x$-axis
of the line $3y = 4x - 5$.  **[3 marks]**

_____

_____

**4** Work out the gradient and intercepts on the $y$-axis and $x$-axis
of the line $4(\frac{1}{2}y + 1) - 3(2 - 3x) = 5$.  **[3 marks]**

_____

_____

**Total marks _____ /10**

## Algebra 43: Use linear graphs to find approximate solutions to simultaneous linear equations

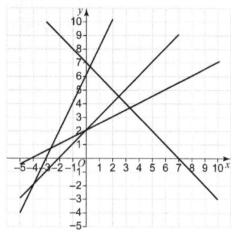

1   Use the graphs to work out the solution to the simultaneous equations.   **[2 marks]**

$y = x + 2$

$y = 2x + 6$

_____

2   Use the graphs to work out the solution to the simultaneous equations.   **[2 marks]**

$y = x + 2$

$y = 7 - x$

_____

3   Use the graphs to work out the solution to the simultaneous equations.   **[2 marks]**

$y = 2x + 6$

$x + y = 7$

_____

4   Use the graphs to work out the solution to the simultaneous equations.   **[2 marks]**

$y = \frac{1}{2}x + 2$

$y = 2x + 6$

_____

5   Use the graphs to work out the solution to the simultaneous equations.   **[2 marks]**

$2y = x + 4$

$x + y = 7$

_____

**Total marks** _____ /10

44                    Algebra

# Algebra 44: Generate terms of a sequence from a term-to-term rule

`No calculator`

**1** Work out the next two terms of this sequence. **[1 mark]**

3, 5, 7, 9, 11, …

_____

**2** Work out the next two terms of this sequence. **[1 mark]**

3.5, 4.6, 5.7, 6.8, 7.9, …

_____

**3** Work out the next two terms of this sequence. **[1 mark]**

21, 16, 11, 6, 1, …

_____

**4** Work out the next two terms of this sequence. **[1 mark]**

0.3, 0, −0.3, −0.6, −0.9, …

_____

**5** Work out the next two terms of this sequence. **[1 mark]**

1, 2, 4, 8, 16, …

_____

**6** Work out the next two terms of this sequence. **[1 mark]**

120, 60, 30, 15, 7.5, …

_____

**7** Work out the next two terms of this sequence. **[2 marks]**

8, 15, 29, 57, 113, …

_____

**8** The term-to-term rule for this sequence is "double and add 2".

2, −2, 6, −10, 22, …

Work out the next two terms of the sequence. **[2 marks]**

_____

**Total marks** _____ /10

# Algebra 45: Generate terms of a sequence from a position-to-term rule

`No calculator`

**1** Work out the 3$^{rd}$ and 10$^{th}$ term in the sequence where the $n^{th}$ term is $n + 5$.                    **[1 mark]**

_____

**2** Work out the 2$^{nd}$ and 5$^{th}$ term in the sequence where the $n^{th}$ term is $2n$.                    **[1 mark]**

_____

**3** Work out the 4$^{th}$ and 9$^{th}$ term in the sequence where the $n^{th}$ term is $3n + 4$.                    **[1 mark]**

_____

**4** Work out the 1$^{st}$ and 12$^{th}$ term in the sequence where the $n^{th}$ term is $20 - 2n$.                    **[1 mark]**

_____

**5** Work out the 5$^{th}$ and 6$^{th}$ term in the sequence where the $n^{th}$ term is $5.3 + 0.6n$.                    **[1 mark]**

_____

**6** Work out the 3$^{rd}$ and 8$^{th}$ term in the sequence where the $n^{th}$ term is $4 - 1.1n$.                    **[1 mark]**

_____

**7** Work out the 20$^{th}$ and 100$^{th}$ term in the sequence where the $n^{th}$ term is $\dfrac{10}{n}$.                    **[2 marks]**

_____

**8** Work out the 3$^{rd}$ and 5$^{th}$ term in the sequence where the $n^{th}$ term is $2n + n$.                    **[2 marks]**

_____

**Total marks _____ /10**

# Algebra 46: Recognise arithmetic sequences and find the $n^{th}$ term

**1** Work out the $n^{th}$ term of this sequence. **[1 mark]**

4, 7, 10, 13, 16, …

_____

**2** Work out the $n^{th}$ term of this sequence. **[1 mark]**

12, 22, 32, 42, 52, …

_____

**3** Work out the $n^{th}$ term of this sequence. **[1 mark]**

21, 32, 43, 54, 65, …

_____

**4** Work out the $n^{th}$ term of this sequence. **[1 mark]**

4.2, 5.4, 6.6, 7.8, 9, …

_____

**5** Work out the $n^{th}$ term of this sequence. **[1 mark]**

90, 85, 80, 75, 70, …

_____

**6** Work out the $n^{th}$ term of this sequence. **[1 mark]**

−4, −10, −16, −22, −28, …

_____

**7** Work out the $n^{th}$ term of this sequence. **[2 marks]**

−5.21, −4.2, −3.19, −2.18, −1.17, …

_____

**8** Work out the $n^{th}$ term of this sequence. **[2 marks]**

$1, \frac{1}{4}, -\frac{1}{2}, -1\frac{1}{4}, -2, \ldots$

_____

**Total marks _____ /10**

# Algebra 47: Recognise geometric sequences and appreciate other sequences that arise

**1** Which of these sequences is a geometric sequence? Write A or B for your answer.  **[1 mark]**

   **A:** 3, 6, 9, 12, …

   **B:** 3, 6, 12, 24, …

   _____

**2** Which of these sequences is a geometric sequence? Write A or B for your answer.  **[1 mark]**

   **A:** 1, −1, 1, −1, 1, …

   **B:** 1, 2, 3, 4, 5, …

   _____

**3** Which of these sequences is a geometric sequence? Write A or B for your answer.  **[1 mark]**

   **A:** 20, 18, 16, 14, 12, …

   **B:** 1, 0.1, 0.01, 0.001, 0.000 1, …

   _____

**4** The first term of a geometric sequence is 1 and the common ratio is 2.  **[1 mark]**

   Write down the first five terms.

   _____

**5** Write down the next two terms in this sequence and describe the sequence.  **[2 marks]**

   2, 3, 5, 7, 11, 13, …

   _____

**6** Write down the next two terms in this sequence and describe the sequence.  **[2 marks]**

   1, 4, 9, 16, 25 …

   _____

**7** Write down the next two terms in this sequence and describe the sequence.  **[2 marks]**

   1, 8, 27, 64, 125 …

   _____

**Total marks _____ /10**

# Ratio, proportion and rates of change 48: Change freely between related units (e.g. time, length, mass)

**1** Change 3 hours 17 minutes to minutes. **[1 mark]**

_____

**2** Change 345 minutes to hours. **[1 mark]**

_____

**3** Change 7.6 kilometres to metres. **[1 mark]**

_____

**4** Change 6700 millimetres to metres. **[1 mark]**

_____

**5** Change 2.1 kilograms to grams. **[1 mark]**

_____

**6** Change 45 000 milligrams to grams. **[1 mark]**

_____

**7** Write the following lengths in order of size, smallest first. **[2 marks]**

40 mm, 40 m, 0.000 4 km, 400 cm

_____

**8** Write the following lengths in order of size, smallest first. **[2 marks]**

0.01 years, 4 days, 100 hours, 3600 minutes

_____

**Total marks _____ /10**

# Ratio, proportion and rates of change 49: Change freely between related compound units (e.g. area, volume/capacity)

No calculator

**1** Change 2 m$^2$ to cm$^2$. [1 mark]

_____

**2** Change 4 768 mm$^2$ to cm$^2$. [1 mark]

_____

**3** Change 1.7 km$^2$ to m$^2$. [1 mark]

_____

**4** Change 2 780 000 cm$^2$ to m$^2$. [1 mark]

_____

**5** Change 2.1 litres to cm$^3$. [1 mark]

_____

**6** Change 45 000 mm$^3$ to cm$^3$. [1 mark]

_____

**7** Write the following areas in order of size, smallest first. [2 marks]

0.006 km$^2$, 600 cm$^2$, 60 m$^2$, 6 000 000 mm$^2$

_____

**8** Write the following areas in order of size, smallest first. [2 marks]

50 000 000 mm$^3$, 5 000 000 cm$^3$, 0.5 m$^3$, 0.000 000 5 km$^3$

_____

**Total marks** _____ /10

# Ratio, proportion and rates of change 50: Use scale factors, scale diagrams and maps

**1** A line, 2.5 centimetres long is enlarged with a scale factor of 2. [1 mark]

Write down the length of the new line.

_____

**2** A circle with radius 9 centimetres is enlarged with a scale factor of $\frac{1}{3}$. [1 mark]

Write down the radius of the new circle.

_____

**3** A triangle with angles of 50°, 60° and 70° is enlarged with a scale factor of 3. [1 mark]

Write down the angles of the enlarged triangle.

_____

**4** A regular hexagon with side length 6 cm is enlarged to a regular hexagon with side length 24 cm. [1 mark]

Write down the scale factor of the enlargement.

_____

**5** A circle with diameter 24 cm is enlarged to a circle diameter 3 cm. [1 mark]

Write down the scale factor of the enlargement.

_____

**6** A line measures 2 cm on a map with a scale of 1 : 100. [1 mark]

Work out the actual distance of the line.

_____

**7** The distance between two towns is 5 km. [2 marks]

Work out the distance this is on a map with a scale of 1 : 100 000. Give your answer in centimetres.

_____

**8** The distance between two schools on a map with a scale of 1 : 25 000 is 8 cm. [2 marks]

Work out the actual distance this represents. Give your answer in kilometres.

_____

Total marks _____ /10

# Ratio, proportion and rates of change 51: Express one quantity as a fraction of another

**1** Write 5 kg as a fraction of 10 kg in its simplest form. **[1 mark]**

_____

**2** Write 40 cm as a fraction of 60 cm in its simplest form. **[1 mark]**

_____

**3** Write 48 cm² as a fraction of 80 cm² in its simplest form. **[1 mark]**

_____

**4** Write 7 kg as a fraction of 3 kg in its simplest form. **[1 mark]**

_____

**5** Write 50 cm³ as a fraction of 4 cm³ in its simplest form. **[1 mark]**

_____

**6** Write 36p as a fraction of £1.44 in its simplest form. **[1 mark]**

_____

**7** Write 20 minutes as a fraction of 2 hours in its simplest form. **[2 marks]**

_____

**8** Write 2 cm as a fraction of 8 mm in its simplest form. **[2 marks]**

_____

**Total marks _____ /10**

# Ratio, proportion and rates of change 52: Use ratio notation, including reduction to simplest form

**1**  Write this ratio in its simplest form.                                                          **[1 mark]**

8 : 10

_____

**2**  Write this ratio in its simplest form.                                                          **[1 mark]**

35 : 49

_____

**3**  Write this ratio in its simplest form.                                                          **[1 mark]**

$3 : \dfrac{1}{2}$

_____

**4**  Write this ratio in its simplest form.                                                          **[1 mark]**

$\dfrac{2}{3} : \dfrac{3}{4}$

_____

**5**  Write this ratio in its simplest form.                                                          **[1 mark]**

£5 : 40p

_____

**6**  Write this ratio in its simplest form.                                                          **[1 mark]**

4.2 metres : 60 centimetres

_____

**7**  Write this ratio in its simplest form.                                                          **[2 marks]**

1.5 metres : 3000 millimetres : 30 centimetres

_____

**8**  Write this ratio in its simplest form.                                                          **[2 marks]**

750 grams : 3 kilograms : 0.06 tonnes

_____

Total marks _____ /10

# Ratio, proportion and rates of change 53: Divide a given quantity in a given ratio

**1** Divide 60 pence in the ratio 3 : 1.

_____

[1 mark]

**2** Divide £5 in the ratio 3 : 7.

_____

[1 mark]

**3** Divide 4 kilograms in the ratio 5 : 3.

_____

[1 mark]

**4** Divide 12 metres in the ratio 17 : 7.

_____

[1 mark]

**5** Divide 0.8 kg in the ratio 7 : 9.

_____

[1 mark]

**6** Divide 3 hours in the ratio 5 : 4.

_____

_____

[1 mark]

**7** Divide £6 in the ratio 5 : 8 : 12.

_____

[2 marks]

**8** Divide 3 hours 20 minutes in the ratio 19 : 5 : 16.

_____

_____

[2 marks]

**Total marks _____ /10**

# Ratio, proportion and rates of change 54: Express the division of a quantity into two parts as a ratio

**1** £6 is divided into two parts. [2 marks]

The first part is £2.

Work out the ratio of the two parts in its simplest form.

_____

**2** 5 metres of wool is divided into two parts. [2 marks]

The first part is 75 centimetres long.

Work out the ratio of the two parts in its simplest form.

_____

**3** 3.2 kilograms of apples is divided into two parts. [2 marks]

The second part is 600 grams.

Work out the ratio of the two parts in its simplest form.

_____

**4** A person works for 200 days in a normal year. [2 marks]

Work out ratio of days worked to days not worked.

Give your answer in its simplest form.

_____

**5** A student attends school from 08:40 until 15:20. [2 marks]

There are eight 45-minute lessons. The rest of the time is free.

Work out the ratio of lesson-time : free-time in its simplest form.

_____

Total marks _____ /10

# Ratio, proportion and rates of change 55: Express a multiplicative relationship between two quantities as a ratio or a fraction

No calculator

1  $y = 3x$. Write down the value of $\dfrac{x}{y}$.

[1 mark]

_____

2  $y = 3x$. Write down the value of $x : y$.

[1 mark]

_____

3  $2y = 5x$. Write down the value of $\dfrac{x}{y}$.

[1 mark]

_____

4  $2y = 5x$. Write down the value of $x : y$.

[1 mark]

_____

5  In a class of students, there are twice as many girls as boys.

[1 mark]

Write down the ratio (number of girls) : (number of boys).

_____

6  In another class of students, there are two girls for every three boys.

[1 mark]

Write down the fraction $\dfrac{\text{number of boys}}{\text{number of girls}}$.

_____

7  In a box of 12 eggs, there are three brown eggs, the others are white.

[2 marks]

Write down the fraction $\dfrac{\text{number of brown eggs}}{\text{number of white eggs}}$ in its simplest form.

_____

8  Jack and Jill drank a total of 3.6 litres of water.

[2 marks]

Jill drank 0.6 litres more than Jack.

Write down the ratio (amount Jill drank) : (amount Jack drank) in its simplest form.

_____

**Total marks** _____ /10

# Ratio, proportion and rates of change 56: Solve problems involving percentage increase

1  Write down the multiplier when an amount is increased by 40%. **[1 mark]**

_____

2  Write down the multiplier when an amount is increased by 6%. **[1 mark]**

_____

3  Write down the multiplier when an amount is increased by 152%. **[1 mark]**

_____

4  Increase £32 by 26%. **[1 mark]**

_____

5  Increase 4.7 metres by 3%. **[1 mark]**

_____

6  Increase 82 kilograms by 12.3%. **[1 mark]**

_____

7  Increase £5.72 by 264%. **[2 marks]**

_____

8  Increase 5 tonnes by 8%, then increase the new amount by 18%. **[2 marks]**

_____

**Total marks _____ /10**

# Ratio, proportion and rates of change 57: Solve problems involving percentage decrease

Calculator allowed

**1** Write down the multiplier when an amount is decreased by 60%. [1 mark]

_____

**2** Write down the multiplier when an amount is decreased by 4%. [1 mark]

_____

**3** Write down the multiplier when an amount is decreased by 0.2%. [1 mark]

_____

**4** Decrease £54 by 42%. [1 mark]

_____

**5** Decrease 4.3 metres by 7%. [1 mark]

_____

**6** Decrease 1.3 tonnes by 99%. [1 mark]

_____

**7** Decrease 17 kilograms by 7%, then decrease the new amount by 80%. [2 marks]

_____

**8** Work out the percentage decrease that is equivalent to a decrease of 6% followed by a decrease of 40%. [2 marks]

_____

Total marks _____ /10

# Ratio, proportion and rates of change 58: Solve problems involving percentages by finding the original amount

1 A dress costs £15 after a 25% increase. Work out the original cost. [1 mark]

_____

2 An object has a mass of 2.4 kilograms after a 40% decrease. Work out the original mass. [1 mark]

_____

3 The area of a metal sheet that is 1.2 m² after a 140% increase. Work out the original area. [1 mark]

_____

4 The length of a lawn is 8.7 metres after a 42% decrease. Work out the original length of the lawn. [1 mark]

_____

5 A fish has a mass of 14 kilograms after an 8% increase. Work out the original mass. Give your answer to the nearest kilogram. [1 mark]

_____

6 In a sale, the price of a coat is reduced by 16%. The sale price is £48.72. Work out the price before the sale. [1 mark]

_____

7 An article is reduced in price by 20% in a sale. Work out the percentage increase on the sale price to bring the price back to the original price. [2 marks]

_____

8 An article is increased in mass by 50%. Calculate the percentage decrease on the increased mass to bring it back to the original mass. [2 marks]

_____

Total marks _____ /10

# Ratio, proportion and rates of change 59: Solve problems involving simple interest

**1** £40 is invested for 2 years at 5% simple interest. Work out the total interest. **[1 mark]**

_____

**2** €750 is invested for 5 years at 2.6% simple interest. Work out the total interest. **[1 mark]**

_____

**3** Work out the rate of simple interest if £200 earns £18 simple interest in 2 years. **[1 mark]**

_____

**4** Work out the rate of simple interest if $350 earns $21 simple interest in 3 years. **[1 mark]**

_____

**5** Work out the number of years that £400 is invested at 4% simple interest to earn £112 in interest. **[1 mark]**

_____

**6** Work out the number of years €520 is invested at 2.1% simple interest to earn €32.76 in interest. **[1 mark]**

_____

**7** Work out the original amount invested if interest of £84 is earned over 7 years at 3% simple interest. **[2 marks]**

_____

**8** Work out the original amount invested if interest of $17.28 is earned over 6 years at 0.9% simple interest. **[2 marks]**

_____

Total marks _____ /10

# Ratio, proportion and rates of change 60: Solve problems involving direct and inverse proportion

**1** 5 litres of petrol costs £6. Work out the cost of 7 litres of petrol. **[1 mark]**

_____

**2** 2.5 kilograms of potatoes costs £1.90. Work out the cost of 4 kilograms of potatoes. **[1 mark]**

_____

**3** 5 reams of A4 paper costs £13.95. Work out the cost of 3 reams of A4 paper. **[1 mark]**

_____

**4** I have enough money to buy 18 calculators at £5 each.

Work out the number of calculators I can buy if the price is £6 each. **[1 mark]**

_____

**5** $m$ is directly proportional to $n$. When $m = 5$, $n = 45$.

Work out $n$ when $m = 7$. **[1 mark]**

_____

**6** $p$ is directly proportional to $q$. When $p = 6.4$, $q = 13.44$.

Work out $p$ when $q = 4.2$. **[1 mark]**

_____

**7** $r$ is inversely proportional to $s$. When $r = 5$, $s = 24$.

Work out $s$ when $r = 15$. **[2 marks]**

_____

**8** $v$ is inversely proportional to $w$. When $v = 16$, $w = 100$.

Work out $v$ when $w = 64$. **[2 marks]**

_____

Total marks _____ /10

# Ratio, proportion and rates of change 61: Use compound units such as speed, unit pricing, and density

Calculator allowed

1 Work out the average speed of a car that travels 168 miles in 3 hours.

[1 mark]

_____

2 An athlete runs at an average speed of 8.5 m/s in 7 seconds.
Work out the distance that he runs.

[1 mark]

_____

3 An aircraft travels 5100 km at an average speed of 450 km/h. Work out the time taken.

[1 mark]

_____

4 Work out the density of 7.6 grams of gold that has a volume of 0.4 cm$^3$.

[1 mark]

_____

5 Work out the mass of 3.1 cm$^3$ of silver that has a density of 10.5 g/cm$^3$.

[1 mark]

_____

6 Work out the volume of 7.5 grams of platinum that has a density of 21.5 g/cm$^3$.

[1 mark]

_____

7 Two rolls of toilet tissue cost £1.49. 15 rolls of the same toilet tissue cost £11.20.
Work out which is the better value.

[2 marks]

_____

_____

_____

8 Brand A of paint costs £8 for 2.5 litres and covers an area of 2.5 m$^2$ per litre.
Brand B of paint costs £15 for 5 litres and covers an area of 2.4 m$^2$ per litre.
Which brand offers the better value for money?

[2 marks]

_____

_____

_____

**Total marks _____ /10**

# Geometry and measures 62: Apply the formulae to calculate perimeter and area of triangles

1 Calculate the perimeter and area of this triangle. **[2 marks]**

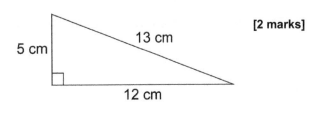

_____  _____

2 Calculate the perimeter and area of this triangle. **[2 marks]**

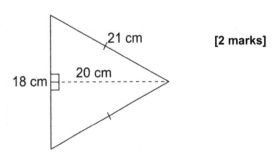

_____  _____

3 Calculate the perimeter and area of this triangle. **[2 marks]**

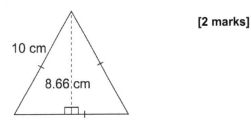

_____  _____

4 Calculate the perimeter and area of the shaded triangle. **[2 marks]**

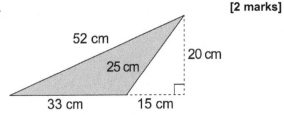

_____  _____

5 The area of this right-angled triangle is 60 cm². 

Calculate the perimeter of the triangle. **[2 marks]**

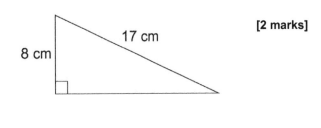

_____  _____

**Total marks _____ /10**

# Geometry and measures 63: Apply the formulae to calculate perimeter and area of parallelograms

**1** Calculate the perimeter and area of this rectangle.

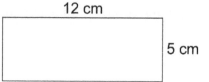

12 cm

5 cm

[2 marks]

_____  _____

**2** Calculate the perimeter and area of this parallelogram.

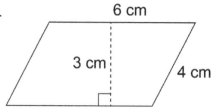

6 cm

3 cm

4 cm

[2 marks]

_____  _____

**3** Calculate the perimeter and area of this parallelogram.

$AB = 2.8c$

$BC = 5.3$ cm

$AC = 4.5$ cm

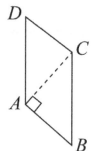

[2 marks]

_____  _____

**4** Calculate the perimeter and area of this parallelogram.

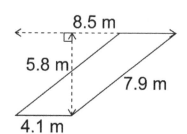

8.5 m

5.8 m

7.9 m

4.1 m

[2 marks]

_____  _____

**5** The area of this parallelogram is 39 cm².

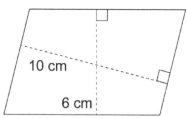

10 cm

6 cm

[2 marks]

The perpendicular distance between one pair of parallel sides is 10 cm.

The perpendicular distance between the other pair of parallel sides is 6 cm.

Calculate the perimeter of the parallelogram.

_____

**Total marks** _____ /10

# Geometry and measures 64: Apply the formulae to calculate perimeter and area of trapezia

1   Calculate the perimeter and area of this trapezium.      **[2 marks]**

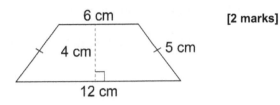

_____   _____

2   Calculate the perimeter and area of this trapezium.      **[2 marks]**

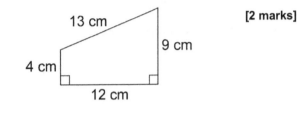

_____   _____

3   Calculate the area of this trapezium.      **[2 marks]**

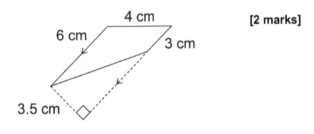

_____

4   The area of this trapezium is 12 cm².

Work out its perimeter.      **[2 marks]**

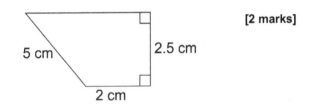

_____

5   The area of this trapezium is 380 cm².

Work out its perimeter.      **[2 marks]**

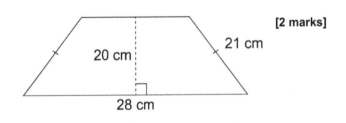

_____

Total marks _____ /10

# Geometry and measures 65: Apply the properties of special types of quadrilaterals

**1** Write down the missing lengths of this kite.

Write down the size of the lettered angle.

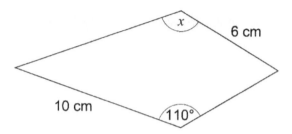

**[2 marks]**

_____

**2** Calculate area of this kite.

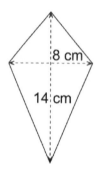

**[2 marks]**

_____

**3** The perimeter of a square is 36.4 cm. Calculate the area of the square. **[2 marks]**

_____

**4** The length of one side of this rhombus is 6 cm.

Work out its perimeter.

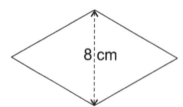

**[1 mark]**

_____

**5** Work out the perimeter of this symmetrical quadrilateral.

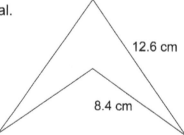

**[2 marks]**

_____

**6** This is an isosceles trapezium.

Work out the size of the lettered angles.

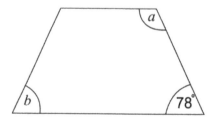

**[1 mark]**

_____

**Total marks _____ /10**

# Geometry and measures 66: Apply the formula to calculate volume of cuboids

**1** Calculate the volume of this cuboid.

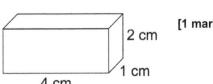

[1 mark]

2 cm
1 cm
4 cm

_____

**2** Calculate the volume of this cuboid.

[1 mark]

7 cm
2 cm
3 cm

_____

**3** Calculate the volume of this cuboid.

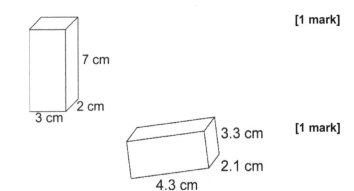

3.3 cm
2.1 cm
4.3 cm

[1 mark]

_____

**4** The volume of this cuboid is 72 m³.

Work out the missing length.

4 m
3 m
?

[1 mark]

_____

**5** The volume of this cuboid is 18 m³.

Work out the missing length.

3.6 m
?
2.5 m

[1 mark]

_____

**6** The volume of a cube is 64 m³. Work out the length of one edge of the cube.

[1 mark]

_____

**7** The volume of this cuboid is 441 cm³. The shaded face is a square of side 4.2 cm.

Work out the height of the cuboid.

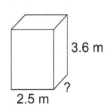

4.2 cm

[2 marks]

_____

**8** The volume of this cuboid is 475 m³. The shaded face is a square.

Work out the length of a side of the square.

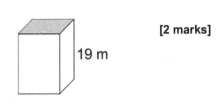

19 m

[2 marks]

_____

**Total marks** _____ /10

# Geometry and measures 67: Apply the formulae to calculate volume of prisms including cylinders

**1** The shaded area of this prism is 16 cm². **[1 mark]**

Calculate the volume.

_____

**2** The shaded area of this tent is 3.6 m³. The cross-section of the tent is the same along its 3 m length. **[1 mark]**

Work out the volume of the tent.

_____

**3** Calculate the volume of the prism. **[2 marks]**

_____

**4** Calculate the volume of the prism. **[2 marks]**

_____

**5** Work out the volume of this cylinder. **[2 marks]**

Give your answer as a multiple of $\pi$.

_____

**6** The volume of this cylindrical biscuit is 80 cm³. **[2 marks]**

The radius is 5 cm.

Calculate the height.

_____

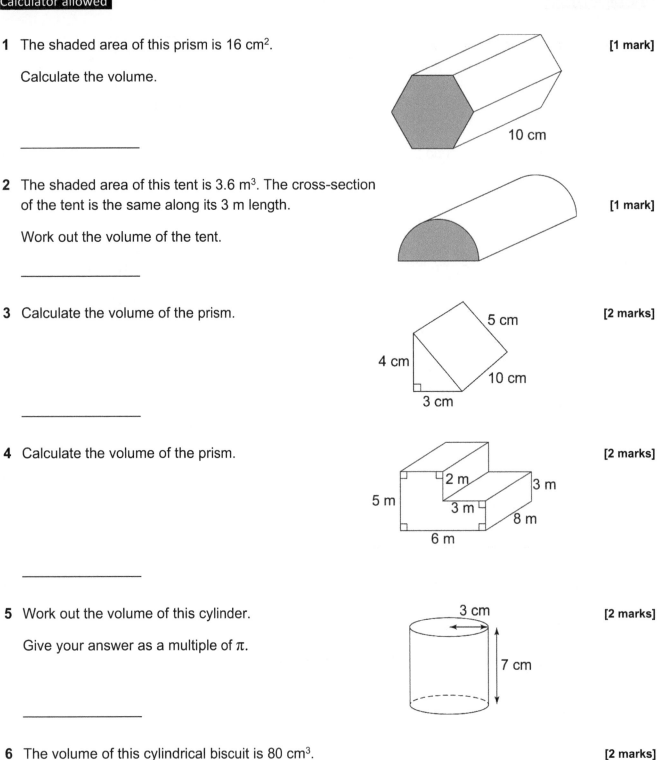

**Total marks _____ /10**

# Geometry and measures 68: Calculate the circumference of circles and perimeter of composite shapes

**1** Work out the circumference of this circle.

Give your answer as a multiple of π.

_____

[1 mark]

6 cm

**2** Work out the circumference of this circle.

Give your answer as a multiple of π.

_____

[1 mark]

4 m

**3** Calculate the circumference of this circle.

Write your answer to 2 decimal places.

_____

[1 mark]

4.7 cm

**4** Calculate the circumference of this circle.

Write your answer to 3 significant figures.

_____

[1 mark]

0.6 m

**5** The circumference of a circle is 42 cm. Calculate its diameter to 1 decimal place.

_____

[1 mark]

**6** The circumference of a circle is 2.89 m. Calculate its radius to 2 significant figures.

_____

[1 mark]

**7** This shape is made from a rectangle and a semicircle.

Calculate the perimeter.

_____

5 cm

10 cm

[2 marks]

**8** This shape has two semicircular arcs.

Calculate the perimeter of the shape.

_____

2 cm

7 cm

[2 marks]

**Total marks _____ /10**

# Geometry and measures 69: Calculate areas of circles and composite shapes

Calculator allowed

1 Calculate the area of this circle.

  Give your answer as a multiple of π.

  _____

  [1 mark]

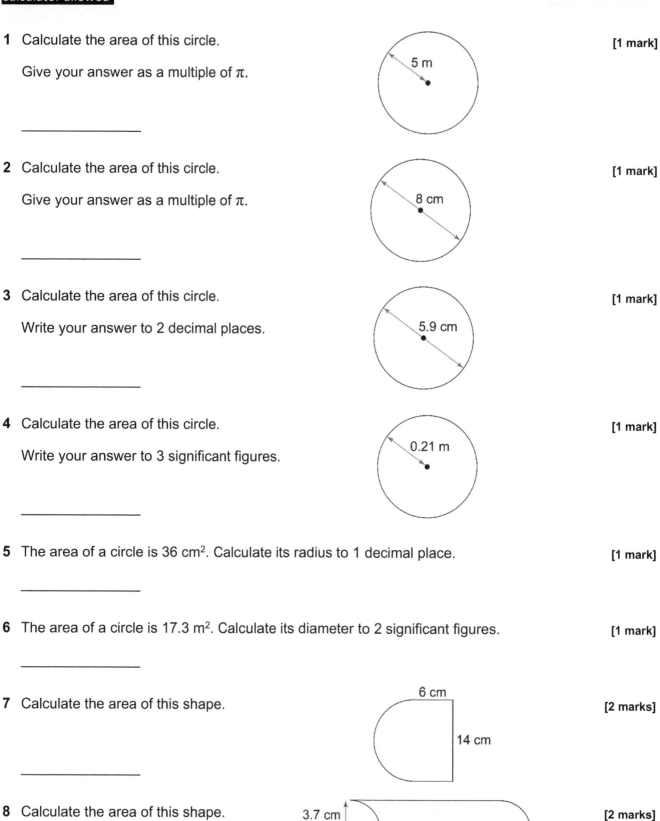

2 Calculate the area of this circle.

  Give your answer as a multiple of π.

  _____

  [1 mark]

3 Calculate the area of this circle.

  Write your answer to 2 decimal places.

  _____

  [1 mark]

4 Calculate the area of this circle.

  Write your answer to 3 significant figures.

  _____

  [1 mark]

5 The area of a circle is 36 cm². Calculate its radius to 1 decimal place.

  _____

  [1 mark]

6 The area of a circle is 17.3 m². Calculate its diameter to 2 significant figures.

  _____

  [1 mark]

7 Calculate the area of this shape.

  _____

  [2 marks]

8 Calculate the area of this shape.

  _____

  [2 marks]

Total marks _____ /10

# Geometry and measures 70: Measure line segments and angles in geometric figures, including interpreting scale drawings

**1** Measure the length of side $AB$ in centimetres.

Measure angle $ABC$ in degrees.

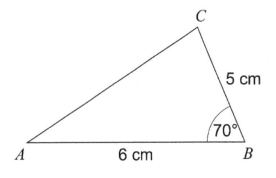

_____

_____

**2** Measure the length of side $DE$ in centimetres.

Measure the length of side $EF$ in millimetres.

Measure angle $DEF$ in degrees.

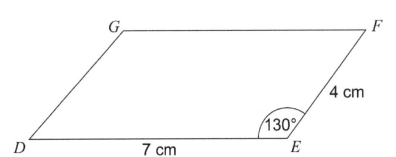

_____

_____

_____

**[2 marks]**

**[3 marks]**

**3** This is a scale drawing of a garden.

Measure the side $JK$ and work out the actual length of the garden side $JK$.

Measure the side $KL$ and work out the actual length of the garden side $KL$.

Measure angle $JKL$ and write down the actual angle in the garden this represents.

**[5 marks]**

### Scale 1 cm to 2 m

_____

_____

_____

_____

_____

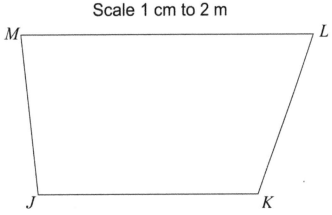

Total marks _____ /10

# Geometry and measures 71: Describe using conventional terms and notations: points, lines, parallel lines, perpendicular lines, right angles, regular polygons, and other polygons that are reflectively and rotationally symmetric

**1** This is a regular pentagon.                                          **[3 marks]**

Write down the side opposite to angle $ABC$.

Write down the number of lines of symmetry of the pentagon.

Write down the order of rotational symmetry of the pentagon.

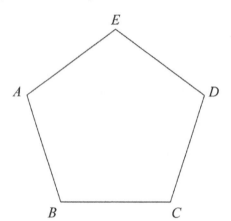

**2** This is a regular octagon.                                           **[7 marks]**

Write down the side opposite side $EF$.

Write down the number of lines of symmetry of the octagon.

Use the vertices to name two lines of symmetry of the octagon.

Write down the order of rotational symmetry of the octagon.

Write down the side that is parallel to side $KL$.

Use vertices to name a line that is perpendicular to side $FG$.

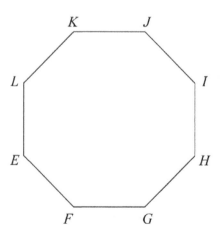

Total marks _____ /10

# Geometry and measures 72: Use the standard convention for labelling triangles and use the basic congruence criteria for triangles (SSS, SAS, ASA, RHS)

Calculator allowed

**1** Write down the number of the triangle that is correctly labelled

[1 mark]

 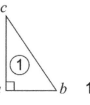 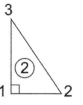  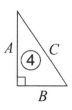 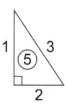

_____

**2** Write down 'YES' if these two triangles are congruent, 'NO' if they are not.

[1 mark]

_____

**3** Write down 'YES' if these two triangles are congruent, 'NO' if they are not.

[1 mark]

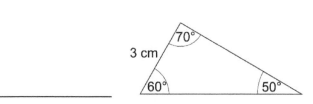 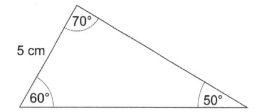

_____

**4** Write down the reason why these two triangles are congruent.

[1 mark]

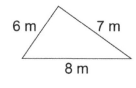 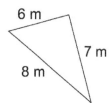

_____

**5** Write down the reason why these two triangles are congruent.

[1 mark]

 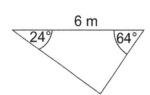

_____

**6** Write down the reason why these two triangles are congruent. **[1 mark]**

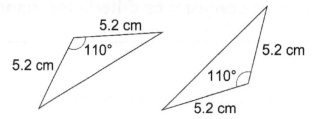

_____

**7** Triangle $ABC$ and triangle $DEF$ are congruent [SAS]. **[2 marks]**

$AB$ = 5 cm, angle $ABC$ = 40°, $BC$ = 7 cm.

Sketch triangle $DEF$.

**8** Triangle $LMN$ and triangle $PQR$ are congruent [RHS]. **[2 marks]**

Angle $RPQ$ = 90°, $RQ$ = 9.1 cm and $PQ$ = 5.2 cm.

Sketch triangle $LMN$.

**Total marks _____ /10**

# Geometry and measures 73: Identify and describe translations

Use this grid to answer questions 1 to 6.

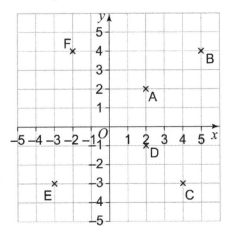

1  Describe the transformation that maps A to B. [1 mark]

_____

2  Describe the transformation that maps E to F. [1 mark]

_____

3  Describe the transformation that maps F to B. [1 mark]

_____

4  Describe the transformation that maps B to F. [1 mark]

_____

5  Describe the transformation that maps A to D. [1 mark]

_____

6  Describe the transformation that maps C to E. [1 mark]

_____

Use this grid to answer questions 7 to 8.

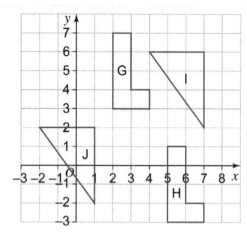

**7** Describe the transformation that maps G to H. **[2 marks]**

_____

**8** Describe the transformation that maps I to J. **[2 marks]**

_____

**Total marks _____ /10**

# Geometry and measures 74: Identify and describe reflections

Use this grid to answer questions 1 to 6.

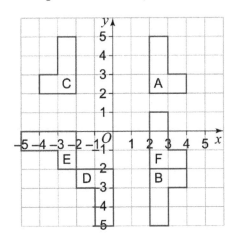

**1** Describe the transformation that maps shape A to shape B.

[1 mark]

_____

**2** Describe the transformation that maps shape A to shape C.

[1 mark]

_____

**3** Describe the transformation that maps shape B to shape D.

[2 marks]

_____

**4** Describe the transformation that maps shape B to shape F.

[2 marks]

_____

**5** Describe the transformation that maps shape D to shape E.

[2 marks]

_____

**6** Describe the transformation that maps shape B to shape C.

[2 marks]

_____

**Total marks** _____ /10

# Geometry and measures 75: Identify and describe rotations

No calculator

Use this grid to answer questions 1 to 5.

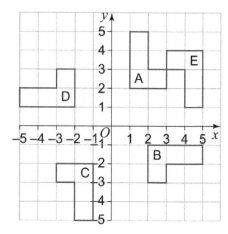

1   Describe the transformation that maps shape A to shape B.                    **[2 marks]**

_____

2   Describe the transformation that maps shape A to shape C.                    **[2 marks]**

_____

3   Describe the transformation that maps shape B to shape D.                    **[2 marks]**

_____

4   Describe the transformation that maps shape A to shape D.                    **[2 marks]**

_____

5   Describe the transformation that maps shape A to shape E.                    **[2 marks]**

_____


**Total marks** _____ /10

# Geometry and measures 76: Apply the properties of angles at a point, angles at a point on a straight line, vertically opposite angles

**1** Work out the size of the lettered angle.

130° a

[1 mark]

_____

**2** Work out the size of the lettered angle.

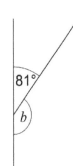

81° b

[1 mark]

_____

**3** Work out the size of the lettered angle.

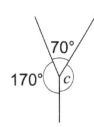

70° 170° c

[1 mark]

_____

**4** Work out the size of the lettered angle.

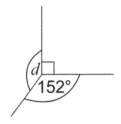

d 152°

[1 mark]

_____

**5** Write down the size of the lettered angle.

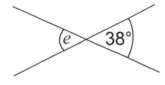

e 38°

[1 mark]

_____

**6** Write down the size of the lettered angle.

f 18°

[1 mark]

_____

**7** Write down the size of the lettered angles.                    **[2 marks]**

_____

_____

**8** Write down the size of the lettered angles.                    **[2 marks]**

_____

_____

**Total marks _____ /10**

# Geometry and measures 77: Understand and use alternate and corresponding angles on parallel lines

**1** Write down whether the angles shown are ALTERNATE or CORRESPONDING angles.     **[1 mark]**

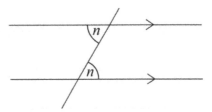

_____

**2** Write down whether the angles shown are ALTERNATE or CORRESPONDING angles.     **[1 mark]**

_____

**3** Write down the size of angle $a$, giving a reason.     **[1 mark]**

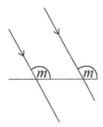

_____

**4** Write down the size of angle $b$, giving a reason.     **[1 mark]**

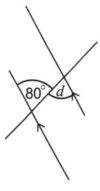

_____

**5** Write down the size of angle $c$, giving a reason.     **[1 mark]**

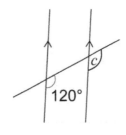

_____

**6**  Write down the size of angle $d$, giving a reason.  **[1 mark]**

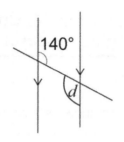

_____

**7**  Write down the size of angles $e$ and $f$, giving reasons.  **[2 marks]**

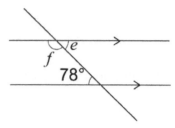

_____

_____

_____

**8**  Write down the size of angles $g$ and $h$, giving reasons.  **[2 marks]**

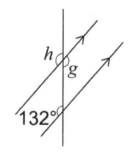

_____

_____

_____

Total marks _____ /10

# Geometry and measures 78: Use the sum of angles in a triangle (e.g. to deduce and use the angle sum in any polygon)

**1** Work out the size of angle *m*.

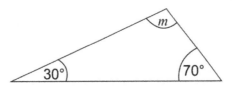

[1 mark]

_____

**2** Work out the size of angle *n*.

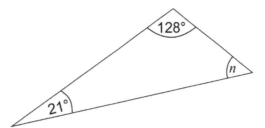

[1 mark]

_____

**3** Work out the size of angle *p*.

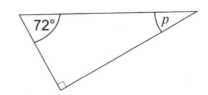

[1 mark]

_____

**4** Work out the size of angle *q*.

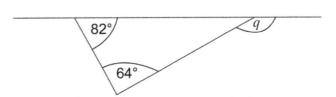

[1 mark]

_____

**5** Work out the size of angle *r*.

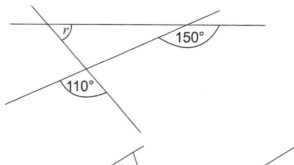

[1 mark]

_____

**6** Work out the size of angle *s*.

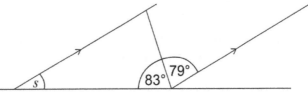

[1 mark]

_____

**7** Work out the angle sum in a hexagon.

[2 marks]

_____

**8** The angle sum of a polygon is 1800°. Work out the number of sides on the polygon.

[2 marks]

_____

Total marks _____ /10

83 Geometry and measures

# Geometry and measures 79: Use Pythagoras' Theorem

1  Calculate the length $a$.

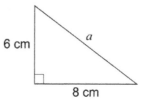

[1 mark]

6 cm  
$a$  
8 cm

_____

2  Calculate the length $b$.

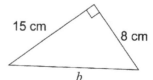

[1 mark]

15 cm  
8 cm  
$b$

_____

3  Calculate the length $c$.

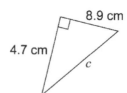

[1 mark]

8.9 cm  
4.7 cm  
$c$

_____

4  Calculate the length $d$.

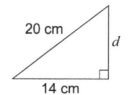

[1 mark]

20 cm  
$d$  
14 cm

_____

5  Calculate the length $e$.

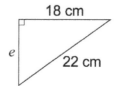

[1 mark]

18 cm  
$e$  
22 cm

_____

6  Calculate the length $f$.

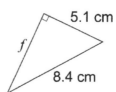

[1 mark]

5.1 cm  
$f$  
8.4 cm

_____

7  Test Pythagoras' Theorem to decide if a triangle with sides of length
   4.5 cm, 10 cm and 10.9 cm is right-angled.

[2 marks]

_____

_____

8  Calculate the length $x$

[2 marks]

9.2 cm  
4.3 cm  
$x$  
5.1 cm

_____

**Total marks _____ /10**

# Geometry and measures 80: Know the formulae for the trig ratios and apply them to find angles

**1** Complete the ratio for a right-angled triangle: $\sin \theta = \dfrac{?}{?}$.  [1 mark]

_____

**2** Write down the value of $\cos \theta$ for this triangle.  [1 mark]

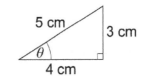

_____

**3** Write down the value of $\tan \theta$ for this triangle.  [1 mark]

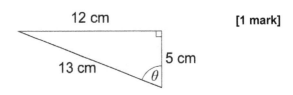

_____

**4** Calculate the size of angle $g$ to the nearest degree.  [1 mark]

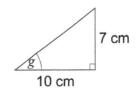

_____

**5** Calculate the size of angle $\theta$ to the nearest degree.  [1 mark]

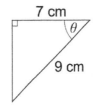

_____

**6** Calculate the missing angle to 2 significant figures.  [1 mark]

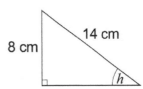

_____

**7** Calculate the missing angle to 1 decimal place.  [2 marks]

_____

**8** Calculate the missing angle to 1 decimal place.  [2 marks]

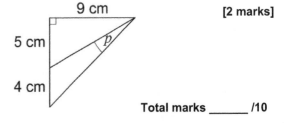

Total marks _____ /10

# Geometry and measures 81: Know the formulae for the trig ratios and apply them to find lengths

1  Write down which of the following is the correct equation for the length $x$ in this diagram.　**[1 mark]**

$x = 10 \sin 50°$, $x = 10 \cos 50°$, $x = \dfrac{10}{\tan 50°}$, $x = \dfrac{10}{\cos 50°}$

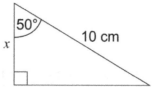

_____

2  Write down which of the following is the correct equation for the length $y$ in this diagram.　**[1 mark]**

$y = 8 \tan 40°$, $y = 8 \cos 40°$, $y = \dfrac{8}{\cos 40°}$, $y = \dfrac{8}{\tan 40°}$

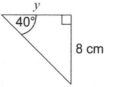

_____

3  Write down which of the following is the correct equation for the length $z$ in this diagram.　**[1 mark]**

$z = 7 \tan 24°$, $z = \dfrac{7}{\tan 24°}$, $z = \dfrac{7}{\sin 24°}$, $z = 7 \sin 40°$

_____

4  Calculate the length $a$ to 3 significant figures.　**[1 mark]**

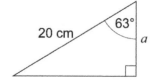

_____

5  Calculate the length $b$ to 3 significant figures.　**[1 mark]**

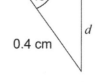

_____

6  Calculate the length $d$ to 3 significant figures.　**[1 mark]**

_____

**7** Calculate the length $e$ to 3 significant figures.

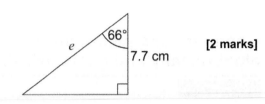

[2 marks]

_____

**8** Calculate the length $f$ to 3 significant figures.

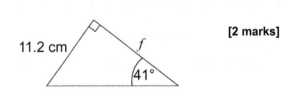

[2 marks]

_____

**Total marks** _____ **/10**

# Geometry and measures 82: Interpret mathematical relationships both algebraically and geometrically

**1** The length of one edge of a cube is 5 cm.  **[2 marks]**

Work out the total length of all the edges.

Work out the total surface area of the cube.

_____

_____

**2** The width of a rectangle is $s$ cm.  **[2 marks]**

The length of the rectangle twice the width.

Write down an expression for the area of the rectangle.

Write down an expression for the perimeter of the rectangle.

_____

_____

**3** The length of one edge of a cube is $n$ cm.  **[3 marks]**

Write down an expression for the total length of all the edges.

Write down an expression for the volume of the cube.

Write down an expression for the total surface area of the cube.

_____

_____

_____

**4** The total length of all the edges of a cube is $p$ cm.  **[3 marks]**

Write down an expression for the length of one edge.

Write down an expression for the surface area of one face of the cube.

Write down an expression for the total surface area of the cube.

_____

_____

_____

**Total marks _____ /10**

# Probability 83: Analyse the frequency of outcomes of simple probability experiments involving randomness, fairness, equally and unequally likely outcomes, using appropriate language and the 0–1 probability scale

No calculator

**1** Write down the probability of an impossible event happening.   **[2 marks]**

Write down the probability of a certain event happening.

_____

**2** Amika throws a coin 10 times. Here are her results for landing on heads (H) and tails(T).   **[3 marks]**

   H  H  T  T  H  T  T  H  H  H

Use the results to write down the probability the coin lands on heads.

Use the results to write down the probability the coin lands on tails.

Do you think it is a fair coin? Write a reason for your answer.

_____

_____

_____

**3** Rajiv puts 100 marbles in a bag. He records the number of each colour but forgot

to write down the number of green marbles. Here is his table.   **[2 marks]**

| Colour | Red | Blue | Yellow | Green |
|--------|-----|------|--------|-------|
| Number | 30  | 20   | 24     |       |

If he picks one marble at random, write down the probability it is blue.

If he picks one marble at random, work out the probability it is green.

_____

_____

**4** Here is a spinner.   **[3 marks]**

Is the arrow equally likely to land on each number?

Write a reason for your answer.

Write down the probability that the arrow lands on 1.

If the arrow is spun 100 times, how many times would you expect it to land on 0?

_____

_____

**Total marks _____ /10**

# Probability 84: Understand that the probabilities of all possible outcomes sum to 1

No calculator

1 The probability of a fair coin landing on heads is $\frac{1}{2}$.

   **[1 mark]**

   Write down which of the following are NOT the correct ways to write this.

   P(Head) = 50%     P(Head) = evens     P(Head) = 0.5     P(Head) = 1 : 1     P(Head) = 50-50

   _____

2 The probability Jen answers this question is 0.8.

   **[1 mark]**

   Write down the probability Jen does not answer this question

   _____

3 The probability Joe does not do his homework tomorrow is 1.

   **[1 mark]**

   Write down the probability Joe does his homework tomorrow.

   _____

4 The probability I will watch TV tonight is $\frac{2}{7}$.

   **[1 mark]**

   Write down the probability that I will not watch TV tonight.

   _____

5 The probability I will send an email tomorrow is 98%.

   **[1 mark]**

   Write down the probability I will not send an email tomorrow.

   _____

6 There are brown, red and blue stones in a bag.

   **[1 mark]**

   This table shows the probability of me picking one at random.

   | Colour | Brown | Red | Blue |
   |---|---|---|---|
   | Probability | 0.4 | 0.5 | |

   Calculate the probability I pick a blue stone.

   _____

**7** There are green, yellow, black and white stones in a bag. [2 marks]

This table shows the probability of choosing one at random.

| Colour | Green | Yellow | Black | White |
|---|---|---|---|---|
| Probability | $\frac{1}{3}$ | | $\frac{5}{12}$ | $\frac{1}{6}$ |

Calculate the probability of choosing a yellow stone.

_____

**8** A biased spinner has the numbers 3, 4, 5 and 6 on it. [2 marks]

The spinner is spun.

This table shows the probability of landing on a particular number.

| Card | 3 | 4 | 5 | 6 |
|---|---|---|---|---|
| Probability | | $\frac{1}{4}$ | $\frac{1}{5}$ | $\frac{1}{6}$ |

Calculate the probability it lands on 3.

_____

Total marks _____ /10

91

# Probability 85: Enumerate sets and unions/intersections of sets using tables

**1** Write down all the outcomes when two fair coins are thrown. **[1 mark]**

_____

**2** Write down all the outcomes in a table when one fair coin is thrown and one fair dice is rolled.

**[1 mark]**

**3** For lunch Jay can have egg (E) or ham (H) or cheese (C) in her sandwiches and a drink of apple juice (A) or peach juice (P). **[1 mark]**

Write down all her possible lunches in a table.

**4** For dinner Ali can choose pasty (P) or spaghetti (S) or fish (F) with beans (B) or carrots (C). **[1 mark]**

Write down all his possible lunches in a table.

**5** This spinner is spun twice and the scores are added together. **[1 mark]**

Write down all the possible totals.

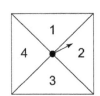

_____

**6** A fair dice is rolled twice and the difference between the scores rolled is recorded.　　　**[1 mark]**

Write down all the possible results.

_____

**7** Write down in a table all the outcomes when three fair coins are thrown.　　　**[2 marks]**

**8** Write down in a table all the possible meals if you have a starter, main and dessert from this menu.　　　**[2 marks]**

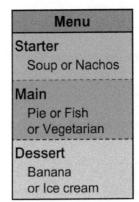

**Menu**

**Starter**
Soup or Nachos

**Main**
Pie or Fish
or Vegetarian

**Dessert**
Banana
or Ice cream

Total marks _____ /10

# Probability 86: Enumerate sets and unions/intersections of sets using grids

No calculator

Use the following information to answer the questions.

In a class of 31 students, 18 are boys. Out of 7 left-handed students in the class, 4 are girls.

|  | Boy | Girl | Total |
|---|---|---|---|
| **Left-handed** | E | D | C |
| **Right-handed** | J | H | G |
| **Total** | B | F | A |

**1** Write down the number that should be written at A. **[1 mark]**

_____

**2** Write down the number that should be written at B. **[1 mark]**

_____

**3** Write down the number that should be written at C. **[1 mark]**

_____

**4** Write down the number that should be written at D. **[1 mark]**

_____

**5** Write down the number that should be written at E. **[1 mark]**

_____

**6** Write down the number that should be written at F. **[1 mark]**

_____

**7** Write down the number that should be written at G. **[1 mark]**

_____

**8** Write down the number that should be written at H. **[1 mark]**

_____

**9** Write down the number that should be written at J. **[1 mark]**

_____

**10** Write down the probability of choosing a right-handed girl at random from this class. **[1 mark]**

_____

Total marks _____ /10

# Probability 87: Enumerate sets and unions/intersections of sets using Venn diagrams

Use the following to answer the questions.

This fair spinner is spun. The Venn diagram shows the two sets for the spinner 'arrow landing on an odd number' (labelled Odd) and 'arrow landing on a prime number' (labelled Prime).

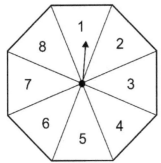
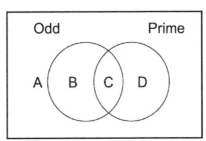

1   Write down the outcomes that should be written in region A.                                    **[1 mark]**

_____

2   Write down the outcomes that should be written in region B.                                    **[1 mark]**

_____

3   Write down the outcomes that should be written in region C.                                    **[1 mark]**

_____

4   Write down the outcomes that should be written in region D.                                    **[1 mark]**

_____

5   Write down the probability that the outcome is not an odd number.                              **[1 mark]**

_____

6   Write down the probability that the outcome is not an odd prime number.                        **[1 mark]**

_____

7   Write down the probability that the outcome is even and not a prime number.                    **[2 marks]**

_____

8   Write down the probability that the outcome is odd and not a prime number.                     **[2 marks]**

_____

Total marks _____ /10

# Probability 88: Construct theoretical possibility spaces for single and combined experiments with equally likely, mutually exclusive outcomes and use these to calculate theoretical probabilities

`No calculator`

Here are three fair spinners A, B and C.

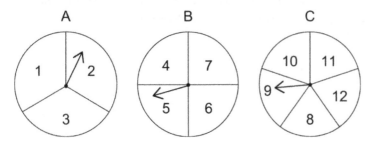

1  Spinner A is spun.                                                                              **[1 mark]**

Write down the possible outcomes.

_____

2  Spinner A is spun.                                                                              **[1 mark]**

Write down the probability that the arrow lands on an odd number.

_____

3  Spinners A and B are spun.                                                                      **[1 mark]**

Write down the possible outcomes.

_____

_____

_____

4  Spinners A and B are spun.                                                                      **[1 mark]**

Write down the probability that both arrows land on prime numbers.

_____

5  Spinners B and C are spun.                                                                      **[1 mark]**

Write down the possible outcomes.

_____

_____

_____

Probability

**6** Spinners B and C are spun. **[1 mark]**

Write down the probability that both arrows land on a number greater than 6.

_____

**7** Spinners A and C are spun. **[1 mark]**

Write down the possible outcomes.

_____

_____

_____

_____

**8** Spinners A and C are spun. **[1 mark]**

Write down the probability that both arrows land on square numbers.

_____

**9** Spinners A, B and C are spun. **[2 marks]**

Work out the probability that all the arrows land on a multiple of 3.

_____

**Total marks _____ /10**

# Statistics 89: Construct tables, charts and diagrams

No calculator

The students in a class were asked, "What is your favourite school subject?".

Here are the results.

| Subject | Tally |
|---------|-------|
| English | ЖІ ІІІ |
| PE | ІІІІ |
| Maths | ЖІ ЖІ ІІ |
| Science | ІІІІ |
| Other | ІІ |

1  Draw a pictogram to show this data.                                    [3 marks]

2  Draw a bar chart to show this data.                                    [3 marks]

3  Draw a pie chart to show this data.                                    [4 marks]

Total marks _____ /10

# Statistics 90: Interpret tables, charts and diagrams

Use the bar chart to answer questions 1 to 3.

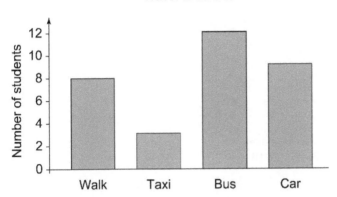

Travel to school

1  Write down the number of students who walk to school.                    **[1 mark]**

   _____

2  Write down the number of students who come by car.                       **[1 mark]**

   _____

3  Write down the total number of students shown in the bar chart.          **[2 marks]**

   _____

Use the pie chart to answer questions 4 and 5.

Use of social media by 50 people

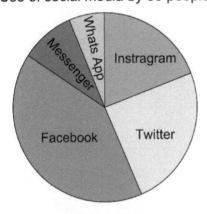

4  Write down the most popular social media.                                **[1 mark]**

   _____

5  Write down the least popular social media.                               **[1 mark]**

   _____

Use the following graph to answer questions 6 to 8.

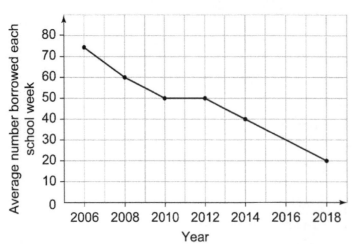

School library books borrowed

6 Estimate the average number of books borrowed each school week in 2013. [1 mark]

_____

7 There are 20 school weeks in a year. Estimate the number of books were borrowed in 2007.

[2 marks]

_____

8 The library closed at the end of 2018. Use the graph to give a possible reason. [1 mark]

_____

**Total marks _____ /10**

# Statistics 91: Interpret appropriate graphical representation involving discrete, continuous and grouped data

No calculator

Use the frequency diagram to answer questions 1 to 3. It shows the times a class of students spent on homework one night.

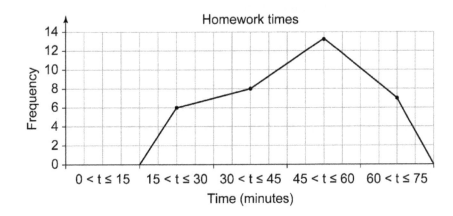

Homework times

1  Write down the number of students who spent between 45 and 60 minutes on their homework.

[1 mark]

_____

2  Write down the minimum time a student could have spent on their homework.          [1 mark]

_____

3  Write down the number of students in the class.          [1 mark]

_____

Use this graph showing the mean monthly temperature for two cities to answer questions 4 to 6

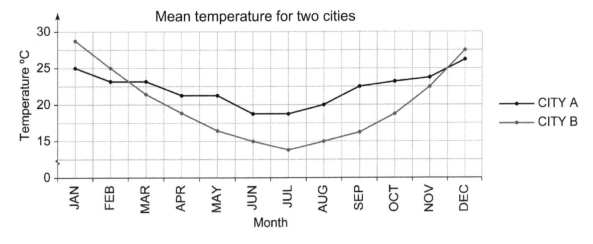

4  Write down the city that has the lower mean monthly temperature.          [1 mark]

_____

**5** Write down the number of months of the year that the temperature in city A is lower than in city B.

[1 mark]

_____

**6** Work out the difference in mean temperatures for the two cities in July.

[1 mark]

_____

Use the pie chart to answer questions 7 to 9

An ice cream seller sold 720 ice creams. The pie chart shows the proportions of the flavour of ice cream sold.

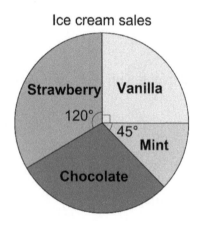

Ice cream sales

**7** Work out the number of vanilla ice creams sold.

[1 mark]

_____

**8** Work out the number of strawberry ice creams sold.

[1 mark]

_____

**9** Work out the number of chocolate ice creams sold.

[2 marks]

_____

Total marks _____ /10

# Statistics 92: Calculate median, mean, mode and range

No calculator

**1** Write down the median for this list.                                        **[1 mark]**

7, 4, 3, 3, 9, 6, 5

_____

**2** Write down the median for this list.                                        **[1 mark]**

4, 5, 6, 7, 8, 9, 9, 9, 9, 10

_____

**3** Write down the mode for this list.                                          **[1 mark]**

4, 5, 6, 7, 8, 9, 9, 9, 9, 10

_____

**4** Write down the range of the numbers in this list.                           **[1 mark]**

4, 5, 6, 7, 8, 9, 9, 9, 9, 10

_____

**5** Work out the mean from this list.                                           **[1 mark]**

3, 7, 20, 20, 10

_____

**6** Work out the mean from this list.                                           **[1 mark]**

0.3, 0.7, 2, 2, 1, 0.6

_____

**7** One number is missing from this list.                                       **[2 marks]**

7, 4, 3, 6, 9

The range of numbers in the complete list is 7. Write down the two possible values for
the missing number.

_____

**8** The mean and the median of the numbers in this list are the same. Work out the value of $x$.  **[2 marks]**

3, 8, 7, 5, $x$, 12, 1

_____

**Total marks _____ /10**

# Statistics 93: Interpret scatter graphs of bivariate data; recognise correlation

`No calculator`

Use the scatter graphs to answer questions 1 to 3.

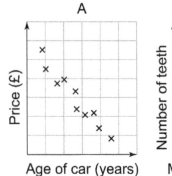 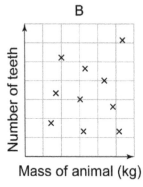 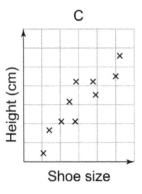

**1** Write down which graph (A, B or C) shows positive correlation. **[1 mark]**

_____

**2** Write down which graph (A, B or C) shows negative correlation. **[1 mark]**

_____

**3** Write down which graph (A, B or C) shows no correlation. **[1 mark]**

_____

Use the following scatter graph to answer questions 4 to 8.

This scatter graph shows the marks of 12 students in two tests.

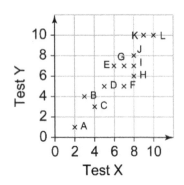

**4** Write down what type of correlation the scatter graph shows. **[1 mark]**

_____

**5** Write down the letter of the student who scored most marks in total. **[1 mark]**

_____

**6** Write down what student C scored in test X. [1 mark]

_____

**7** Write down which two students scored a total of 14. [2 marks]

_____

**8** Write down which two students' scores in the tests differed most. [2 marks]

_____

**Total marks _____ /10**

## Number 1: Answers

| | | |
|---|---|---|
| 1 | 7039 | [1 mark] |
| 2 | 58.006 | [1 mark] |
| 3 | 7.4 | [1 mark] |
| 4 | 20.063 | [1 mark] |
| 5 | Three hundred or 300 | [1 mark] |
| 6 | Five thousandths or 0.005 | [1 mark] |
| 7 | Forty thousand or 40 000 | [1 mark] |
| 8 | Two ten-thousandths | [1 mark] |

9  Five tenths, thirty-six hundredths, **[2 marks]**
eight hundredths, seventy-four
thousandths
or 0.5, 0.36, 0.08, 0.074
**[1 mark]** for three in the correct order
ignoring fourth value
e.g. 0.5, 0.36, 0.074, 0.08

## Number 2: Answers

1  0, 3, 5, 10, 12, 13 **[1 mark]**

2  0.345, 3.398, 3.4, 3.402, 3.411 **[1 mark]**

3  $\dfrac{1}{4}, \dfrac{1}{2}, \dfrac{2}{3}, \dfrac{3}{4}, \dfrac{7}{8}$ **[1 mark]**

4  Any fraction answer between $\dfrac{3}{8}$
and $\dfrac{1}{2}$ e.g. $\dfrac{4}{10}$ **[1 mark]**

5  Any number starting with 0.71…,
excluding 0.71 **[1 mark]**

6  $6\dfrac{1}{4}, 6\dfrac{1}{8}, 2\dfrac{3}{4}, 2\dfrac{1}{2}, \dfrac{4}{7}$ **[1 mark]**

7  2.333, $2\dfrac{1}{3}$, $2\dfrac{2}{5}$, 2.41, $2\dfrac{9}{20}$ **[2 marks]**

**[1 mark]** for any four in correct order

8  Greatest 5,991 **[1 mark]**
Least 5,001 **[1 mark]**

## Number 3: Answers

1  −13, −11, −1, 0, 2, 4 **[1 mark]**

2  −2.374, −2.304, −2.3, −2.29, −0.236 **[1 mark]**

3  $-\dfrac{4}{5}, -\dfrac{3}{4}, -\dfrac{1}{2}, -\dfrac{1}{3}, -\dfrac{1}{4}$ **[1 mark]**

4  Any answer between $-\dfrac{4}{5}$ and $-\dfrac{1}{2}$
e.g. $-\dfrac{5}{7}$ **[1 mark]**

5  Any number starting with −0.0…
excluding 0 **[1 mark]**

6  $3\dfrac{1}{4}, 3\dfrac{1}{8}, \dfrac{3}{2}, -1\dfrac{1}{2}, -1\dfrac{3}{4}$ **[1 mark]**

7  $-5\dfrac{2}{5}, -5.62, -5.666, -5\dfrac{2}{3}, -5\dfrac{17}{20}$ **[2 marks]**

**[1 mark]** for any four in correct order

8  Greatest −3003 **[1 mark]**
Least −4994 **[1 mark]**

## Number 4: Answers

1  5 < 7 (or 7 > 5) **[1 mark]**

2  −4 < −3.6 (or −3.6 > −4) **[1 mark]**

3  $0.7 = \dfrac{7}{10}$ **[1 mark]**

4  7 − 5 > 5 − 7 **[1 mark]**

5  $6\dfrac{1}{3}$ > 6.333 **[1 mark]**

6  $2\dfrac{1}{4}$ > −2.25 **[1 mark]**

7  1, 2, 3, 4, 5 **[2 marks]**
**[1 mark]** for one error or omission

8  −3, −2, −1 **[2 marks]**
**[1 mark]** for one error or omission

## Number 5: Answers

1  2, 5, 11, 19 **[1 mark]**

2  3, 33, 39, 51 **[1 mark]**
(advise students that the sum of the
digits is a multiple of 3)

3  3, 1 **[1 mark]**
(advise students that they only need
to consider the units digit)

4  97 **[1 mark]**

5  $2^2 \times 3 \times 11$ or $2 \times 2 \times 3 \times 11$ **[1 mark]**

6  $3^3 \times 5$ or $3 \times 3 \times 3 \times 5$ **[1 mark]**

7  $2^3 \times 3^2 \times 5$ or $2 \times 2 \times 2 \times 3 \times 3 \times 5$ **[2 marks]**
**[1 mark]** for factors 2, 3 and 5 seen

8  37, 73 **[2 marks]**

## Number 6: Answers

| | | |
|---|---|---|
| 1 | 6 | [1 mark] |
| 2 | 20 | [1 mark] |
| 3 | 15 | [1 mark] |
| 4 | 6 | [1 mark] |
| 5 | 4 | [1 mark] |
| 6 | 42 | [1 mark] |

7  12 **[2 marks]**
**[1 mark]** for any other multiple of 12
that gives a HCF of 12, e.g. 36, 60, 84…

**8** 210      [2 marks]

[1 mark] for any other multiple of 210

## Number 7: Answers

**1** 15      [1 mark]

**2** 70      [1 mark]

**3** 60      [1 mark]

**4** 420      [1 mark]

**5** 60      [1 mark]

**6** 900      [1 mark]

**7** 6      [2 marks]

[1 mark] for 150

**8** 8      [2 marks]

[1 mark] for any other number that gives LCM of 360 (e.g. 24, 40, 72, 360)

## Number 8: Answers

**1** −8      [1 mark]

**2** (+)6      [1 mark]

**3** −15      [1 mark]

**4** (+)4      [1 mark]

**5** −20      [1 mark]

**6** −4      [1 mark]

**7** −19      [2 marks]

[1 mark] for −16 seen

**8** 12      [2 marks]

[1 mark] for 6 seen

## Number 9: Answers

**1** 66.2(0)      [1 mark]

**2** 5.43      [1 mark]

**3** −0.35      [1 mark]

**4** 70      [1 mark]

**5** −0.88      [1 mark]

**6** 2.4      [1 mark]

**7** 0.026 78      [2 marks]

[1 mark] for digits 2678 seen e.g. 0.267 8

**8** 15.6      [2 marks]

[1 mark] for digits 156 seen e.g. 15.6 or 1.56

## Number 10: Answers

**1** $\frac{11}{15}$      [1 mark]

**2** $\frac{17}{28}$      [1 mark]

**3** $-\frac{1}{12}$      [1 mark]

**4** $3\frac{5}{8}$      [1 mark]

**5** $1\frac{7}{10}$      [1 mark]

**6** $2\frac{13}{14}$      [1 mark]

**7** $-\frac{1}{20}$      [2 marks]

[1 mark] for common denominator used with at least two correct fractions,

e.g. two from $\frac{20}{60}$, $\pm\frac{35}{60}$ or $\frac{12}{60}$

**8** $6\frac{41}{60}$      [2 marks]

[1 mark] for $4\frac{3}{4}$ or $\pm1\frac{14}{15}$

## Number 11: Answers

**1** $\frac{2}{15}$      [1 mark]

**2** $5\frac{1}{4}$ or $\frac{21}{4}$      [1 mark]

**3** $\frac{1}{12}$      [1 mark]

**4** 8      [1 mark]

**5** −2      [1 mark]

**6** $2\frac{1}{2}$ or $\frac{5}{2}$      [1 mark]

**7** $1\frac{83}{160}$ or $\frac{243}{160}$      [2 marks]

[1 mark] for $\frac{27}{32}$ or $\frac{27}{40}$

**8** $1\frac{5}{16}$ or $\frac{21}{16}$      [2 marks]

[1 mark] for $\pm\frac{35}{24}$

## Number 12: Answers

**1** 23      [1 mark]

**2** −1      [1 mark]

**3** $\frac{5}{2}$ or $2\frac{1}{2}$      [1 mark]

**4** 6      [1 mark]

**5** $(4 + 3)^2 = 49$      [1 mark]

**6** 10      [1 mark]

**7** $\sqrt{(55 - 5) \div 2}$      [1 mark]

**8** $1 + 3^2 - (8 + 2) = 0$      [1 mark]

**9** $\frac{1}{10}$ or 0.1      [2 marks]

[1 mark] for 10 as answer to calculation

## Number 13: Answers

1  81 [1 mark]
2  32 [1 mark]
3  100 000 [1 mark]
4  343 [1 mark]
5  10 [1 mark]
6  3 [1 mark]
7  160 [2 marks]

[1 mark] for 32 or 5 seen

8  3.1 [2 marks]

[1 mark] for 31 or 10 seen

## Number 14: Answers

1  $2^3$ [1 mark]
2  $3^2$ [1 mark]
3  $4^3$ [1 mark]
4  $3^4$ [1 mark]
5  $5^4$ [1 mark]
6  $2^9$ [1 mark]
7  $5^3 + 3 = 5 \times 5 \times 5 + 3 = 125 + 3 = 128$

   $2^7 = 2 \times 2 \times 2 \times 2 \times 2 \times 2 \times 2 = 128$

   [1 mark] for showing either side is 128  [2 marks]
8  $2^3 \times 5^3 + 24 = 8 \times 125 + 24 = 1000 + 24 = 1024$

   $2^{10} = 2 \times 2 \times 2 \times 2 \times 2 \times 2 \times 2 \times 2 \times 2 \times 2 = 1024$

   [1 mark] for showing either side is 1024  [2 marks]

## Number 15: Answers

1  36 [1 mark]
2  8 [1 mark]
3  8 and 9 [1 mark]
4  29 and 30 [1 mark]
5  1.414 is a terminating decimal. $\sqrt{2}$ as a decimal goes on for ever without any regular pattern. [1 mark]
6  $\sqrt{0.64} = 0.8$ [1 mark]
7  $\dfrac{\sqrt{25}}{\sqrt[3]{1000}} = \dfrac{11}{15} = 0.5$

   [1 mark] for 5 or 10 seen  [2 marks]
8  e.g. any two from 0.001, 0.008, 0.027, 0.064, 0.125, 0.216, 0.343, 0.512, 0.729 (there are others)

   [1 mark] for each answer  [2 marks]

## Number 16: Answers

1  $3.7 \times 10^3$ [1 mark]
2  $4.6 \times 10^{-2}$ [1 mark]
3  $5 \times 10^0$ [1 mark]
4  470 [1 mark]
5  0.006 2 [1 mark]
6  4.56 [1 mark]
7  $3.1 \times 10^1 = 3.1$ [2 marks]

   [1 mark] for $3.1 \times 10^1$ chosen
8  $2.1 \times 10^{-4} = 0.000\ 21$ [2 marks]

   [1 mark] for $2.1 \times 10^{-4}$ chosen

## Number 17: Answers

1  0.25 [1 mark]
2  0.8 [1 mark]
3  3.875 [1 mark]
4  $\dfrac{2}{5}$ [1 mark]
5  $\dfrac{3}{20}$ [1 mark]
6  $8\dfrac{1}{8}$ [1 mark]
7  $3.4, \dfrac{7}{2}, 3\dfrac{4}{7}, \dfrac{37}{10}, 3\dfrac{3}{4}$ [2 marks]

   [1 mark] for any four in the correct order
8  $\dfrac{58}{10}, \dfrac{45}{8}, 5\dfrac{1}{2}, 5.3, \dfrac{21}{4}$ [2 marks]

   [1 mark] for any four in the correct order

## Number 18: Answers

1  25% [1 mark]
2  50% [1 mark]
3  200% [1 mark]
4  75% [1 mark]
5  10% [1 mark]
6  108% [1 mark]
7  82.1…%

   [1 mark] digits 821…, e.g. 0.821  [2 marks]
8  0.428…% or 0.429%, 0.43%

   [1 mark] for digits 428, 429 or 43 seen, e.g. 0.004 29  [2 marks]

# Number 19: Answers

1  11 out of 15 (73% against 68%)  **[2 marks]**
   **[2 marks]** for 11 out of 15 (working shown)
   **[1 mark]** for either percentage correct

2  51 g in 80 g (64% against 59%)  **[2 marks]**
   **[2 marks]** for 51 g in 80 g (working shown)
   **[1 mark]** for either percentage correct

3  0.2 g in 150 g  **[2 marks]**
   (0.133% against 0.138%)
   **[2 marks]** for 0.2 g in 150 g (working shown)
   **[1 mark]** for either percentage correct

4  £145 on £23 500  **[2 marks]**
   (0.617% against 0.613%)
   **[2 marks]** for £145 on £23 500 (working shown)
   **[1 mark]** for either percentage correct

5  2.9 kg off 42.6 kg  **[2 marks]**
   (6.8% against 7.2%)
   **[2 marks]** for 2.9 kg off 42.6 kg (working shown)
   **[1 mark]** for either percentage correct

# Number 20: Answers

1  gram, kilogram, tonne  **[1 mark]**

2  kilometre, metre, centimetre, millimetre
   **[1 mark]**

3  second, minute, hour, day, week, month, year  **[1 mark]**

4  09:03  **[1 mark]**

5  £17.97  **[1 mark]**

6  Teacher to state height in centimetres **[1 mark]**

7  56 cm  **[2 marks]**
   **[1 mark]** for 144 seen

8  655 g  **[2 marks]**
   **[1 mark]** for 1345 or 345 seen

# Number 21: Answers

1  3.41  **[1 mark]**

2  0.070  **[1 mark]**

3  5.5  **[1 mark]**

4  0.337  **[1 mark]**

5  0.023 4  **[1 mark]**

6  10.68  **[1 mark]**

7  1.465 cm, 1.474 9 cm  **[2 marks]**

**[2 marks]** accept 1.475 cm
**[1 mark]** for one correct

8  33.337 5 cm$^2$  **[2 marks]**
   **[1 mark]** for 6.35 or 5.25 seen

# Number 22: Answers

1  42  **[1 mark]**

2  0.078 1  **[1 mark]**

3  600 000  **[1 mark]**

4  0.230  **[1 mark]**

5  51.08  **[1 mark]**

6  1800  **[1 mark]**

7  80.95 kg, 81.04$\dot{9}$ kg  **[2 marks]**
   **[2 marks]** accept 81.05 kg
   **[1 mark]** for one correct

8  461,000  **[2 marks]**
   **[1 mark]** for 461 160

# Number 23: Answers

1  30  **[1 mark]**

2  10  **[1 mark]**

3  20  **[1 mark]**

4  2500  **[1 mark]**

5  0.000 9  **[1 mark]**

6  1  **[1 mark]**

7  60, he is not correct  **[2 marks]**
   **[2 marks]** for $\frac{3 \times 6}{0.3}$ = 60 shown
   **[1 mark]** for any two correct approximations

8  1,000, she could be correct  **[2 marks]**
   **[2 marks]** for $\frac{8000}{10 \times 0.8}$ = 1000 shown
   **[1 mark]** for any two correct approximations

# Algebra 24: Answers

1  $pq$  **[1 mark]**

2  $4e$  **[1 mark]**

3  $7g$  **[1 mark]**

4  $n^3$  **[1 mark]**

5  $c^2d$  **[1 mark]**

6  $\frac{3m}{5}$ or $0.6m$  **[1 mark]**

7  $3h$  **[2 marks]**

[1 mark] for $2h + h$ seen

8   $7(6a - 5c)$ or $42a - 35c$   [2 marks]

   [1 mark] for $6a - 5c$ seen

## Algebra 25: Answers

1   $m + n$   [1 mark]

2   $r - 60$   [1 mark]

3   $t - s$   [1 mark]

4   $3.5y + 0.5$   [1 mark]

5   $6x, \dfrac{x}{10}$   [1 mark]

6   $\dfrac{p}{8}, \dfrac{p}{10}$   [2 marks]

7   $8n, 2^t n$   [2 marks]

## Algebra 26: Answers

1   17   [1 mark]

2   13   [1 mark]

3   11   [1 mark]

4   51   [1 mark]

5   –2   [1 mark]

6   36   [1 mark]

7   21   [2 marks]

   [1 mark] for –3 or 24 seen

8   8.1   [2 marks]

   [1 mark] for 5.74 or 2.401 or 8.141
   or 8.14 seen

## Algebra 27: Answers

1   24.9   [1 mark]

2   0.71   [1 mark]

3   45.9   [1 mark]

4   52.81   [1 mark]

5   60   [1 mark]

6   77   [1 mark]

7   25.4   [2 marks]

   [1 mark] for 7.05 or 25.38 seen

8   $3\dfrac{1}{3}$ or $\dfrac{10}{3}$   [2 marks]

   [1 mark] for 30 and 9 seen

## Algebra 28: Answers

1   $3x^2y, 4x + 6.4cd$   [1 mark]

2   $y = 4x + 2, V = \dfrac{4}{3}\pi r^3$ (also a formula) [1 mark]

3   $5m - 4n > 6p, 4x \leq 6y - 9$   [1 mark]

4   $-3bc$ (the negative sign is essential)   [1 mark]

5   2, $x$, $2x$ (accept any one of these)   [1 mark]

6   5, $n$, $5n$   [1 mark]

7   Student's own answer – ask a   [2 marks]
   partner to check.

   [1 mark] for an expression with 3 or $x$
   as a common factor

8   Student's own answer – ask a   [2 marks]
   partner to check.

   [2 marks] for a full explanation with
   examples, e.g. an expression is one
   or more terms, e.g. $3xy$ or $3x + 2y$.
   An equation contains an equals sign,
   e.g. $3x = 2$

   [1 mark] for a partial answer, e.g. one
   correct definition with example or
   correct definitions without examples
   as a common factor

## Algebra 29: Answers

1   $4a$   [1 mark]

2   $5c$   [1 mark]

3   $3x + 4y$   [1 mark]

4   $8 - y$ or $-y + 8$   [1 mark]

5   $8w + 5$   [1 mark]

6   $e + 4f$   [1 mark]

7   $a = 6, b = 12$   [2 marks]

8   $c = 14, d = 3$   [2 marks]

## Algebra 30: Answers

1   $3a + 6b$   [1 mark]

2   $2x^2 - x$   [1 mark]

3   $6b2 + 8bc$   [1 mark]

4   $8c - 12c^2$   [1 mark]

5   $2g^2 - g$   [1 mark]

6   $11h - 3h^2$   [1 mark]

7   $6d^2 - 3d - 15$   [2 marks]

   [1 mark] for $6d^2 - 8d$ or $5d - 15$ or
   any two correct terms

8   $14ef - 4e^2 + 2f^2$   [2 marks]

   [1 mark] for $20ef - 4e^2$ or $-6ef + 2f^2$ or
   any two correct terms

## Algebra 31: Answers

**1** $2(2a + 5)$ [1 mark]

**2** $5(3 - 4b)$ [1 mark]

**3** $c(6c + 5)$ [1 mark]

**4** $2d(7 - 9d)$ [1 mark]

**5** $3e(1 + 3e)$ [1 mark]

**6** $f^2(f - 4)$ [1 mark]

**7** $3g(2 + 3g + 7g^2)$ [2 marks]

[1 mark] for $3(2g + 3g^2) + 7g^3)$ or
$g(6 + 9g + 21g^2)$

**8** $2mn(8mn - m^2 + 2n^2)$ [2 marks]

[1 mark] for $mn(16mn - 2m^2 + 4n^2)$ or
$2m(8mn^2 - m^2n + 2n^3)$ or
$2n(8m^2n - m^3 + 2mn^2)$

## Algebra 32: Answers

**1** $a^2 + 5a + 6$ [1 mark]

**2** $b^2 - b - 12$ [1 mark]

**3** $c^2 + c - 30$ [1 mark]

**4** $d^2 - 10d + 21$ [1 mark]

**5** $6e^2 + 7e + 2$ [1 mark]

**6** $8 + 2f - 3f^2$ [1 mark]

**7** $6g^2 - 13g + 6$ [2 marks]

[1 mark] for $6g^2 - 4g - 9g + 6$ (allow one error)

**8** $-6h^2 + 23h - 20$ [2 marks]

[1 mark] for $-6h^2 + 8h + 15h - 20$ (allow one error)

## Algebra 33: Answers

**1** $d = \dfrac{C}{\pi}$ [1 mark]

**2** $r = \sqrt{\dfrac{A}{\pi}}$ [1 mark]

**3** $u = v - at$ [1 mark]

**4** $a = \dfrac{v - u}{t}$ [1 mark]

**5** $u = \sqrt{v^2 - 2as}$ [1 mark]

**6** $F = \dfrac{9c}{5} + 32$ or $F = 1.8C + 32$ [1 mark]

**7** $v = \dfrac{2s}{t} - u$ or $v = 2s - ut$ [2 marks]

[1 mark] for $vt = 2s - ut$ or $2s = ut + vt$

**8** $f = \dfrac{uv}{u + t}$ [2 marks]

[1 mark] for $vf + uf = uv$ or $vf = uv - uf$

## Algebra 34: Answers

**1** $a = 4$ [1 mark]

**2** $b = 3$ [1 mark]

**3** $c = 1.5$ [1 mark]

**4** $d = -1\dfrac{1}{3}$ or $\dfrac{4}{3}$ [1 mark]

**5** $e = 6$ [1 mark]

**6** $f = 7$ [1 mark]

**7** $g = \dfrac{2}{3}$ [2 marks]

[1 mark] for $8 - 6g - 4$

**8** $h = 2$ [2 marks]

[1 mark] for $4 - 18 + 15g$

## Algebra 35: Answers

**1** $j = 6$ [1 mark]

**2** $k = \dfrac{5}{6}$ [1 mark]

**3** $m = 5$ [1 mark]

**4** $n = 12.5$ [1 mark]

**5** $p = -0.5$ [1 mark]

**6** $q = -1$ [1 mark]

**7** $r = -1.25$ [2 marks]

[1 mark] for $12 + 10r$ and $r + 3$ seen

**8** $s = \dfrac{2}{3}$ [2 marks]

[1 mark] for $-6 + 4s$ and $10s + 5$ seen

## Algebra 36: Answers

**1** $(2, 1)$ [1 mark]

**2** $(3, -3)$ [1 mark]

**3** $(-4, -2)$ [1 mark]

**4** $(0, 0)$ [1 mark]

**5** F [1 mark]

**6** $(0, 2)$ [1 mark]

**7** $\left(2, -\dfrac{1}{2}\right)$ [2 marks]

[1 mark] for one correct coordinate

**8** $\left(\dfrac{1}{2}, -\dfrac{1}{2}\right)$ [2 marks]

**[1 mark]** for one correct coordinate **[2 marks]**

## Algebra 37: Answers

1  $x = 2$ **[1 mark]**
2  $y = 4$ **[1 mark]**
3  $y = x$ **[1 mark]**
4  $y = 2x$ **[1 mark]**
5  $y = 4 - x$ **[1 mark]**
6  $y = 1 - 0.5x$ **[1 mark]**
7  Straight line through (0, 3) and gradient 2
   **[1 mark]** for straight line with a gradient of 2 or straight line passing through (0, 3) **[2 marks]**
8  Straight line through (0, 6) and (6, 0)
   **[1 mark]** for straight line with a gradient of −1 or straight line passing through (0, 6) **[2 marks]**

## Algebra 38: Answers

1  C **[1 mark]**
2  $y = x^2$ **[1 mark]**
3  $y = x^2 + 4$ **[1 mark]**
4  $y = 0.5x^2$ **[1 mark]**
5  $y = -x^2$ **[1 mark]**
6  $y = 2 - x^2$ **[1 mark]**
7  A U-shaped curve with vertex at (0, 2)
   **[1 mark]** for U-shape, but (0, 2) not the minimum **[2 marks]**
8  A ∩-shaped curve with vertex at (0, 5)
   **[1 mark]** for ∩-shape, but (0, 5) not the maximum **[2 marks]**

## Algebra 39: Answers

1  $a = b + 3$ **[1 mark]**
2  $c = 2d$ **[1 mark]**
3  $e = f - 5$ **[1 mark]**
4  $g = \dfrac{h}{4}$ **[1 mark]**
5  $5j = k + 2$ **[1 mark]**
6  $\dfrac{m}{n} = p$ **[1 mark]**
7  $\dfrac{q}{2} - 6 = r - 5$ **[2 marks]**

   **[1 mark]** for $\dfrac{q}{2} - 6$ or $r - 5$

8  $7t = \dfrac{1}{b} + 2$ **[2 marks]**

   **[1 mark]** for $7t$ or $\dfrac{1}{b} + 2$

## Algebra 40: Answers

1  Sketch graph of $x = 3$ **[1 mark]**
2  Sketch graph of $y = -1$ **[1 mark]**
3  Sketch graph of $y = 2x$ **[1 mark]**
4  Sketch graph of $y = 3x$ **[1 mark]**
5  Sketch graph of $y = x + 3$ **[1 mark]**
6  Sketch graph of $y = x$ **[1 mark]**
7  Sketch graph of $y = x^2$ **[2 marks]**
   **[1 mark]** for $y = x^2$ seen
8  Sketch graph of $y = x^2 + 2$ **[2 marks]**
   **[1 mark]** for $y = x^2 + 2$ seen

## Algebra 41: Answers

1  $y = 3x + 2$ **[1 mark]**
2  $y = 6x - 10$ **[1 mark]**
3  $y = \dfrac{1}{2}x + 2$ **[1 mark]**
4  $y = \dfrac{5}{4}x - \dfrac{3}{4}$ **[1 mark]**
5  $y = -4x + 20$ **[1 mark]**
6  $y = -\dfrac{3}{4}x - 3$ **[1 mark]**
7  $y = 10x - 15$ **[2 marks]**
   **[1 mark]** for $y - 10x + 15 = 0$
8  $y = -\dfrac{5}{3}x + 5$ **[2 marks]**
   **[1 mark]** for $3y - 8$

## Algebra 42: Answers

1  gradient is $\dfrac{4}{3}$, intercept on $y$-axis is $-\dfrac{5}{3}$, intercept on $x$-axis is $\dfrac{5}{4}$

   **[1 mark]** for gradient,
   **[1 mark]** for intercepts **[2 marks]**

2  gradient is $-\dfrac{2}{3}$, intercept on $y$-axis is $-\dfrac{4}{3}$, intercept on $x$-axis is −2

   **[1 mark]** for gradient,
   **[1 mark]** for intercepts **[2 marks]**

3    gradient is $\dfrac{10}{3}$, intercept on $y$-axis is $\dfrac{11}{3}$,

     intercept on $x$-axis is $-\dfrac{11}{10}$

     **[1 mark]** for gradient,
     **[1 mark]** for each intercept      **[3 marks]**

4    gradient is $-\dfrac{9}{2}$, intercept on $y$-axis is 3.5

     or $\dfrac{7}{2}$, intercept on $x$-axis is $\dfrac{7}{9}$

     **[1 mark]** for gradient,
     **[1 mark]** for each intercept      **[3 marks]**

## Algebra 43: Answers

1   $x = -4, y = -2$      **[2 marks]**

    **[1 mark]** for each correct value

2   $x = 2.5, y = 4.5$      **[2 marks]**

    **[1 mark]** for each correct value

3   $x = \dfrac{1}{3}, y = 6\dfrac{2}{3}$      **[2 marks]**

    **[1 mark]** for each value. Accept answers in the following ranges $(0.2 \le x \le 0.5, 6.5 \le y \le 6.8)$

4   $x = -2\dfrac{2}{3}, y = \dfrac{2}{3}$      **[2 marks]**

    **[1 mark]** for each value. Accept answers in the following ranges $(-2.8 \le x \le -2.5, 0.5 \, y \le 0.8)$

5   $x = 3\dfrac{1}{3}, y = 3\dfrac{2}{3}$      **[2 marks]**

    **[1 mark]** for each value. Accept answers in the following ranges $(3.2 \le x \le 3.5, 3.5 \le y \le 3.8)$

## Algebra 44: Answers

1   13, 15      **[1 mark]**
2   9, 10.1      **[1 mark]**
3   −4, −9      **[1 mark]**
4   −1.2, −1.5      **[1 mark]**
5   32, 64      **[1 mark]**
6   3.75, 1.875      **[1 mark]**
7   225, 449 **[1 mark]** for each      **[2 marks]**
8   −42, 86   **[1 mark]** for each      **[2 marks]**

## Algebra 45: Answers

1   8, 15      **[1 mark]**
2   4, 10      **[1 mark]**
3   16, 31      **[1 mark]**
4   18, −4      **[1 mark]**
5   8.3, 8.9      **[1 mark]**
6   0.7, −4.8      **[1 mark]**
7   0.5, 0.1 **[1 mark]** for each      **[2 marks]**
8   11, 37   **[1 mark]** for each      **[2 marks]**

## Algebra 46: Answers

1   $3n + 1$      **[1 mark]**
2   $10n + 2$      **[1 mark]**
3   $11n + 10$      **[1 mark]**
4   $1.2n + 3$      **[1 mark]**
5   $95 - 5n$      **[1 mark]**
6   $2 - 6n$      **[1 mark]**
7   $-6.22 + 1.01n$      **[2 marks]**

    **[1 mark]** for $1.01n$ seen

8   $1\dfrac{3}{4} - \dfrac{3}{4}n$ or $1.75 - 0.75n$      **[2 marks]**

    **[2 marks]** or equivalent

    **[1 mark]** for $-\dfrac{3}{4}n$ or $-0.75n$ seen

## Algebra 47: Answers

1   B      **[1 mark]**
2   A      **[1 mark]**
3   B      **[1 mark]**
4   1, 2, 4, 8, 16      **[1 mark]**
5   17, 19      **[1 mark]**
    prime numbers      **[1 mark]**
6   36, 49      **[1 mark]**
    square numbers      **[1 mark]**
7   216, 343      **[1 mark]**
    cube numbers      **[1 mark]**

## Ratio, proportion and rates of change 48: Answers

1   197 minutes      **[1 mark]**
2   $5\dfrac{3}{4}$ hours or 5.75 hours      **[1 mark]**
3   7600 metres      **[1 mark]**
4   6.7 metres      **[1 mark]**
5   2100 grams      **[1 mark]**

**6** 45 grams [1 mark]

**7** 40 mm, 0.000 4 km, 400 cm, 40 m

[1 mark] for three lengths in correct
order ignoring fourth length [2 marks]

**8** 3,600 minutes, 0.01 years, 4 days, 100
hours

[1 mark] for three times in correct
order ignoring fourth time [2 marks]

# Ratio, proportion and rates of change 49: Answers

**1** 20 000 cm² [1 mark]

**2** 47.68 cm² [1 mark]

**3** 1 700 000 m² [1 mark]

**4** 278 m² [1 mark]

**5** 2100 cm³ [1 mark]

**6** 45 cm³ [1 mark]

**7** 600 cm², 6 000 000 mm², 60 m², 0.006 km²

[1 mark] for three areas in correct
order ignoring fourth area [2 marks]

**8** 50 000 000 mm³, 0.5 m³, 5 000 000 cm³,
0.000 000 5 km³

[1 mark] for three volumes in correct
order ignoring fourth volume [2 marks]

# Ratio, proportion and rates of change 50: Answers

**1** 5 cm [1 mark]

**2** 3 cm [1 mark]

**3** 50°, 60° and 70° [1 mark]

**4** 4 [1 mark]

**5** $\frac{1}{8}$ [1 mark]

**6** 200 cm or 2 m [1 mark]

**7** 5 cm [2 marks]

[1 mark] for 0.000 05 (km)
or 0.05 m seen

**8** 2 km [2 marks]

[1 mark] for 200 000 (cm)
or 2000 m seen

# Ratio, proportion and rates of change 51: Answers

**1** $\frac{1}{2}$ [1 mark]

**2** $\frac{2}{3}$ [1 mark]

**3** $\frac{3}{5}$ [1 mark]

**4** $\frac{7}{3}$ or $2\frac{1}{3}$ [1 mark]

**5** $\frac{25}{2}$ or $12\frac{1}{2}$ [1 mark]

**6** $\frac{1}{4}$ [1 mark]

**7** $\frac{1}{6}$ [2 marks]

[1 mark] for $\frac{20}{120}$ seen

**8** $\frac{5}{2}$ or $2\frac{1}{2}$ [2 marks]

[1 mark] for $\frac{20}{8}$ seen

# Ratio, proportion and rates of change 52: Answers

**1** 4 : 5 [1 mark]

**2** 5 : 7 [1 mark]

**3** 6 : 1 [1 mark]

**4** 8 : 9 [1 mark]

**5** 25 : 2 [1 mark]

**6** 7 : 1 [1 mark]

**7** 5 : 10 : 1 [2 marks]

[1 mark] for all three in consistent units,
e.g. 1500 mm, (3000 mm), 300 mm
or 1500 : 3000 : 300

**8** 1 : 4 : 80 [2 marks]

[1 mark] for all three in consistent units,
e.g. (750 grams), 3000 grams,
60 000 grams
or 750 : 3000 : 60 000

# Ratio, proportion and rates of change 53: Answers

**1** 45p : 15p [1 mark]

**2** £1.50 : £3.50 [1 mark]

**3** 2.5 kg : 1.5 kg [1 mark]

**4** 8.5 m : 3.5 m [1 mark]

**5** 0.35 kg : 0.45 kg or 350 g : 450 g [1 mark]

**6** 100 minutes : 80 minutes or [1 mark]
1 hour 40 minutes : 1 hour 20 minutes

**7** £1.20 : £1.92 : £2.88 [2 marks]

[1 mark] for 24p seen

**8** 95 minutes : 25 minutes : 80 minutes or
1 hour 35 minutes : 25 minutes : 1 hour 20 minutes

**[1 mark]** for 5 minutes seen                    **[2 marks]**

## Ratio, proportion and rates of change 54: Answers

**1**  1 : 2                                                **[2 marks]**
**[1 mark]** for correct ratio in unsimplified form

**2**  3 : 17                                               **[2 marks]**
**[1 mark]** for correct ratio in unsimplified form

**3**  13 : 3                                               **[2 marks]**
**[1 mark]** for correct ratio in unsimplified form

**4**  40 : 33                                              **[2 marks]**
**[1 mark]** for correct ratio in unsimplified form

**5**  9 : 1                                                **[2 marks]**
**[1 mark]** for correct ratio in unsimplified form

## Ratio, proportion and rates of change 55: Answers

**1**  $\frac{1}{3}$                                         **[1 mark]**

**2**  1 : 3                                                **[1 mark]**

**3**  $\frac{2}{5}$                                         **[1 mark]**

**4**  2 : 5                                                **[1 mark]**

**5**  2 : 1                                                **[1 mark]**

**6**  $\frac{3}{2}$                                         **[1 mark]**

**7**  $\frac{1}{3}$                                         **[2 marks]**
**[1 mark]** for an equivalent fraction

**8**  5 : 7, 1.5 : 2.1                                      **[2 marks]**
**[1 mark]** for unsimplified ratio

## Ratio, proportion and rates of change 56: Answers

**1**  1.4                                                  **[1 mark]**

**2**  1.06                                                 **[1 mark]**

**3**  2.52                                                 **[1 mark]**

**4**  £40.32                                               **[1 mark]**

**5**  4.841 m                                              **[1 mark]**

**6**  92.086 kg                                            **[1 mark]**

**7**  £20.82                                               **[2 marks]**
**[1 mark]** for 20.820 8 or 3.64 seen

**8**  6.372 tonnes                                         **[2 marks]**

**[1 mark]** for 5.4 or 1.08 and 1.18 seen

## Ratio, proportion and rates of change 57: Answers

**1**  0.4                                                  **[1 mark]**

**2**  0.96                                                 **[1 mark]**

**3**  0.998                                                **[1 mark]**

**4**  £31.32                                               **[1 mark]**

**5**  3.999 m                                              **[1 mark]**

**6**  0.013 tonnes or 13 kg                                **[1 mark]**

**7**  3.162 kg                                             **[2 marks]**
**[1 mark]** for 15.81 or 0.92 and 0.2 seen

**8**  43.6%                                                **[2 marks]**
**[1 mark]** for 0.564 or 0.94 and 0.6 seen

## Ratio, proportion and rates of change 58: Answers

**1**  £12                                                  **[1 mark]**

**2**  4 kg                                                 **[1 mark]**

**3**  0.5 m²                                               **[1 mark]**

**4**  15 m                                                 **[1 mark]**

**5**  13 kg                                                **[1 mark]**

**6**  £58                                                  **[1 mark]**

**7**  25%                                                  **[2 marks]**
**[1 mark]** for 0.8 seen

**8**  33% or 33.3% or $33\frac{1}{3}$%                     **[2 marks]**
**[1 mark]** for 1.5 seen

## Ratio, proportion and rates of change 59: Answers

**1**  £4                                                   **[1 mark]**

**2**  €97.50                                               **[1 mark]**

**3**  4.5%                                                 **[1 mark]**

**4**  2%                                                   **[1 mark]**

**5**  7 years                                              **[1 mark]**

**6**  3 years                                              **[1 mark]**

**7**  £400                                                 **[2 marks]**
**[1 mark]** for ÷ (0.03 × 7) seen

**8**  $320                                                 **[2 marks]**
**[1 mark]** for ÷ (0.009 × 6) seen

## Ratio, proportion and rates of change 60: Answers

1  £8.40                                      [1 mark]

2  £3.04                                      [1 mark]

3  £8.37                                      [1 mark]

4  15                                         [1 mark]

5  63                                         [1 mark]

6  2                                          [1 mark]

7  8                                          [2 marks]
   [1 mark] for 120 seen

8  25                                         [2 marks]
   [1 mark] for 1600 seen

## Ratio, proportion and rates of change 61: Answers

1  56 mph                                     [1 mark]

2  59.5 metres                               [1 mark]

3  11 hours 20 minutes                       [1 mark]

4  19 g/cm$^3$                                [1 mark]

5  32.55 grams                               [1 mark]

6  2.86 cm$^3$                                [1 mark]

7  Two rolls are better value: each roll costs
   74.5p.
   15 rolls cost 74.67p to 2 dp for each roll
   or e.g. 30 rolls is 15 lots of 2 rolls and costs
   £22.35,
   and 30 rolls is 2 lots of 15 rolls and costs
   £22.40.
   [1 mark] for valid comparison with no
   or incorrect conclusion                    [2 marks]

8  Brand B is better value: the amount covered
   by £1 worth of paint is 0.8 m$^2$.
   For Brand A the amount covered by £1 worth
   of paint is 0.781 25 m$^2$
   or e.g. Brand A is £16 for a 5 litre can.
   [1 mark] for valid comparison with no
   or incorrect conclusion                    [2 marks]

## Geometry and measures 62: Answers

1  perimeter = 30 cm                          [1 mark]
   area = 30 cm$^2$                           [1 mark]

2  perimeter = 60 cm                          [1 mark]
   area = 180 cm$^2$                          [1 mark]

3  perimeter = 30 cm                          [1 mark]

   area = 43.3 cm$^2$                         [1 mark]

4  perimeter = 110 cm                         [1 mark]
   area = 330 cm$^2$                          [1 mark]

5  40 cm                                      [2 marks]
   [1 mark] for 15 seen

## Geometry and measures 63: Answers

1  perimeter = 34 cm                          [1 mark]
   area = 60 cm$^2$                           [1 mark]

2  perimeter = 20 cm                          [1 mark]
   area = 18 cm$^2$                           [1 mark]

3  perimeter = 16.2 cm                        [1 mark]
   area = 12.6 cm$^2$                         [1 mark]

4  perimeter = 24 cm                          [1 mark]
   area = 23.78 cm$^2$                        [1 mark]

5  20.8 cm                                    [2 marks]
   [1 mark] for 3.9 cm or 6.5 cm seen as the
   lengths of the parallel sides

## Geometry and measures 64: Answers

1  perimeter = 28 cm                          [1 mark]
   area = 36 cm$^2$                           [1 mark]

2  perimeter = 38 cm                          [1 mark]
   area = 78 cm$^2$                           [1 mark]

3  area = 15.75 cm$^2$                        [2 marks]
   [1 mark] for correct calculation seen
   e.g. 4.5 × 3.5

4  perimeter = 17.1 cm                        [2 marks]
   [1 mark] for fourth side = 7.6 cm

5  80 cm                                      [2 marks]
   [1 mark] for side = 10 cm

## Geometry and measures 65: Answers

1  6 cm, 10 cm                                [1 mark]
   110°                                       [1 mark]

2  56 cm$^2$                                  [2 marks]
   [1 mark] for area of one triangle
   of 28 cm$^2$ or 8 × 14 or 112

3  82.81 cm$^2$                               [2 marks]
   [1 mark] for side length of 9.1 cm seen

4  24 cm                                      [1 mark]

5  42 cm                                      [2 marks]

**[1 mark]** for 21 cm seen

**6** $a = 102°, b = 78°$           **[1 mark]**

## Geometry and measures 66: Answers

**1** 8 cm$^3$           **[1 mark]**

**2** 42 cm$^3$           **[1 mark]**

**3** 29.799 cm$^3$ or 29.8 cm$^3$ or 30 cm$^3$     **[1 mark]**

**4** 6 m           **[1 mark]**

**5** 2 m           **[1 mark]**

**6** 4 m           **[1 mark]**

**7** 25 cm           **[2 marks]**
    **[1 mark]** for 4.2 × 4.2 or 17.64 seen

**8** 5 cm           **[2 marks]**
    **[1 mark]** for 475 ÷ 19 or 25 seen

## Geometry and measures 67: Answers

**1** 160 cm$^3$           **[1 mark]**

**2** 10.8 m$^3$           **[1 mark]**

**3** 60 cm$^3$           **[2 marks]**
    **[1 mark]** for cross-section = 6 cm$^2$

**4** 192 m$^3$           **[2 marks]**
    **[1 mark]** for cross-section = 24 cm$^2$

**5** 63$\pi$ cm$^3$           **[2 marks]**
    **[1 mark]** for cross-section = 9$\pi$ cm$^3$

**6** 1.02 cm or 1 cm           **[2 marks]**
    **[1 mark]** for cross-section = 25$\pi$

## Geometry and measures 68: Answers

**1** 6$\pi$ cm           **[1 mark]**

**2** 8$\pi$ m           **[1 mark]**

**3** 14.77 cm           **[1 mark]**

**4** 3.77 m           **[1 mark]**

**5** 13.4 cm           **[1 mark]**

**6** 0.46 m           **[1 mark]**

**7** (20 + 5$\pi$) cm or 35.7 cm        **[2 marks]**
    **[1 mark]** for 5$\pi$ or 10$\pi$ seen

**8** (14+ 4$\pi$) cm or 26.6cm        **[2 marks]**
    **[1 mark]** for 2$\pi$ or 4$\pi$ seen

## Geometry and measures 69: Answers

**1** 25$\pi$ m$^2$           **[1 mark]**

**2** 16$\pi$ cm$^2$           **[1 mark]**

**3** 27.34 cm$^2$           **[1 mark]**

**4** 0.139 m$^2$           **[1 mark]**

**5** 3.4 cm           **[1 mark]**

**6** 4.7 m           **[1 mark]**

**7** 84 + 24.5$\pi$ cm$^2$ or 161 cm$^2$     **[2 marks]**
    **[1 mark]** for 49 × $\pi$ or 24.5 × $\pi$ or 6 × 14
    or 84 seen

**8** 59.94 cm$^2$           **[2 marks]**
    **[1 mark]** for 3.7 × 2 × 8.1

## Geometry and measures 70: Answers

**1** 6 cm           **[1 mark]**
   70°           **[1 mark]**

**2** 7 cm           **[1 mark]**
   40 mm           **[1 mark]**
   130°           **[1 mark]**

**3** 6 cm           **[1 mark]**
   12 m           **[1 mark]**
   4.5 cm           **[1 mark]**
   9 m           **[1 mark]**
   110°           **[1 mark]**

## Geometry and measures 71: Answers

**1** *DE*           **[1 mark]**
   5           **[1 mark]**
   5           **[1 mark]**

**2** *JI*           **[1 mark]**
   8           **[1 mark]**
   Any two of *EI, FJ, GK* or *HL*     **[2 marks]**
   8           **[1 mark]**
   *HG*           **[1 mark]**
   Any one of *LE, KF, JG* or *IH*     **[1 mark]**

## Geometry and measures 72: Answers

**1** 3           **[1 mark]**

**2** NO           **[1 mark]**

**3** NO (they are similar)      **[1 mark]**

**4** SSS      **[1 mark]**

**5** ASA or AA corresponding S      **[1 mark]**

**6** SAS      **[1 mark]**

**7**

**[2 marks]** for correct triangle with labels in correct positions. Any orientation.
**[1 mark]** for correct triangle with no labels. Any orientation.      **[2 marks]**

**8**

**[2 marks]** for correct triangle with labels in correct positions. Any orientation.
**[1 mark]** for correct triangle with no labels. Any orientation.      **[2 marks]**

## Geometry and measures 73: Answers

**1** Translation $\begin{pmatrix} 3 \\ 2 \end{pmatrix}$      **[1 mark]**

**2** Translation $\begin{pmatrix} 1 \\ 7 \end{pmatrix}$      **[1 mark]**

**3** Translation $\begin{pmatrix} 7 \\ 0 \end{pmatrix}$      **[1 mark]**

**4** Translation $\begin{pmatrix} -7 \\ 0 \end{pmatrix}$      **[1 mark]**

**5** Translation $\begin{pmatrix} 0 \\ -3 \end{pmatrix}$      **[1 mark]**

**6** Translation $\begin{pmatrix} 0 \\ -7 \end{pmatrix}$      **[1 mark]**

**7** Translation $\begin{pmatrix} 3 \\ -6 \end{pmatrix}$

**[1 mark]** for each correct value      **[2 marks]**

**8** Translation $\begin{pmatrix} -6 \\ -4 \end{pmatrix}$

**[1 mark]** for each correct value      **[2 marks]**

## Geometry and measures 74: Answers

**1** Reflection in the line $y = 0$ or reflection in the $x$-axis      **[1 mark]**

**2** Reflection in the line $x = 0$ or reflection in the $y$-axis      **[1 mark]**

**3** Reflection in the line $x = 1$

**[1 mark]** for reflection
**[1 mark]** for $x = 1$      **[2 marks]**

**4** Reflection in the line $y = -2$

**[1 mark]** for reflection
**[1 mark]** for $y = -2$      **[2 marks]**

**5** Reflection in the line $y = x$

**[1 mark]** for reflection
**[1 mark]** for $y = x$      **[2 marks]**

**6** Reflection in the line $y = -x$

**[1 mark]** for reflection
**[1 mark]** for $y = -x$      **[2 marks]**

## Geometry and measures 75: Answers

**1** Rotation, 90° clockwise, about (0, 0) or or rotation, 270° anticlockwise, about (0, 0)

**[1 mark]** for angle and direction
**[1 mark]** for centre      **[2 marks]**

**2** Rotation, 180°, about (0, 0)

**[1 mark]** for angle and direction
**[1 mark]** for centre      **[2 marks]**

**3** Rotation, 180°, about (0, 0)

**[1 mark]** for angle and direction
**[1 mark]** for centre      **[2 marks]**

**4** Rotation, 90° anticlockwise, about (0, 0) or rotation, 270° clockwise, about (0, 0)

**[1 mark]** for angle and direction
**[1 mark]** for centre      **[2 marks]**

**5** Rotation, 180°, about (3, 3)

**[1 mark]** for angle and direction
**[1 mark]** for centre      **[2 marks]**

## Geometry and measures 76: Answers

**1** 50°      **[1 mark]**

**2** 99°      **[1 mark]**

**3** 120°      **[1 mark]**

**4** 118° [1 mark]

**5** 38° [1 mark]

**6** 18° [1 mark]

**7** $g = 41°$ [1 mark]

$h = 57°$ [1 mark]

**8** $m = 122°$ [1 mark]

$n = 32°$ [1 mark]

## Geometry and measures 77: Answers

**1** ALTERNATE [1 mark]

**2** CORRESPONDING [1 mark]

**3** 38° corresponding angles (are equal) [1 mark]

**4** 80° alternate angles (are equal) [1 mark]

**5** 120° corresponding angles (are equal) [1 mark]

**6** 140° alternate angles (are equal) [1 mark]

**7** $e = 78°$ alternate angles (are equal) [1 mark]

$f = 102°$ angles on a straight line add to 180° (or supplementary angles add to 180°) [2 marks]

**8** $g = 132°$ alternate angles (are equal) [1 mark]

$h = 132°$ corresponding angles (are equal) (or vertically opposite angles (are equal)) [2 marks]

## Geometry and measures 78: Answers

**1** 80° [1 mark]

**2** 31° [1 mark]

**3** 18° [1 mark]

**4** 146° [1 mark]

**5** 40° [1 mark]

**6** 18° [1 mark]

**7** 720° [2 marks]

[1 mark] for 4 × 180° seen

**8** 12 [2 marks]

[1 mark] for 1800 ÷ 180 or 10 (triangles)

## Geometry and measures 79: Answers

**1** 10 cm [1 mark]

**2** 17 cm [1 mark]

**3** 10.06… cm or 10.1 cm or 10 cm [1 mark]

**4** 14.28… cm or 14.3 cm or 14 cm [1 mark]

**5** 12.6… cm or 13 cm [1 mark]

**6** 6.67… cm or 6.7 cm [1 mark]

**7** $4.5^2 + 10^2 = 120.25$ [2 marks]

$10.9^2 = 118.81$

NOT right-angled

[1 mark] for 120.25 and 118.81 and correct conclusion

**8** 6.3 … cm [2 marks]

[1 mark] for 6.67 cm or 6.7 cm seen as the common side

## Geometry and measures 80: Answers

**1** $\sin \theta = \dfrac{\text{opposite}}{\text{hypotenuse}}$ [1 mark]

**2** $\dfrac{4}{5}$ or 0.8 [1 mark]

**3** $\dfrac{12}{5}$ or 2.4 [1 mark]

**4** 35° [1 mark]

**5** 39° [1 mark]

**6** 35° [1 mark]

**7** 33.4° [2 marks]

[1 mark] for use of tan

**8** 15.9° [2 marks]

[1 mark] for 45° seen

## Geometry and measures 81: Answers

**1** $x = 10\cos 50°$ [1 mark]

**2** $y = \dfrac{8}{\tan 40°}$ [1 mark]

**3** $z = \dfrac{7}{\sin 24°}$ [1 mark]

**4** 9.08 cm [1 mark]

**5** 23.8 cm [1 mark]

**6** 0.302 cm [1 mark]

**7** 18.9 cm [2 marks]

[1 mark] for $\cos 66° = \dfrac{7.7}{e}$

**8** 12.9 cm [2 marks]

[1 mark] for $\tan 41° = \dfrac{11.2}{f}$

# Geometry and measures 82: Answers

**1** 60 cm      **[1 mark]**

   150 cm²      **[1 mark]**

**2** $2s^2$ cm²      **[1 mark]**

   $6s$ cm      **[1 mark]**

**3** $12n$ cm      **[1 mark]**

   $n^3$ cm³      **[1 mark]**

   $6n^2$ cm²      **[1 mark]**

**4** $\dfrac{p}{12}$ cm      **[1 mark]**

   $\dfrac{P^2}{144}$ cm²      **[1 mark]**

   $\dfrac{P^2}{24}$ cm²      **[1 mark]**

# Probability 83: Answers

**1** 0      **[1 mark]**

   1      **[1 mark]**

**2** $\dfrac{3}{5}$ or $\dfrac{6}{10}$ or 0.6 or 60%      **[1 mark]**

   $\dfrac{2}{5}$ or $\dfrac{4}{10}$ or 0.4 or 40%      **[1 mark]**

   e.g. No: the probabilities/outcomes are not the same.
or Yes: the probabilities/outcomes are close      **[1 mark]**

**3** $\dfrac{20}{100}$ or $\dfrac{1}{5}$ or 0.2 or 20%      **[1 mark]**

   $\dfrac{26}{100}$ or $\dfrac{13}{50}$ or 0.26 or 26%      **[1 mark]**

**4** No: as two sectors are 1 or twice as likely to land on 1      **[1 mark]**

   $\dfrac{1}{2}$ or 50%      **[1 mark]**

   25 times      **[1 mark]**

# Probability 84: Answers

**1** P(Head) = evens    P(Head) = 1 : 1
P(Head) = 50–50      **[1 mark]**

**2** 0.2 or $\dfrac{1}{5}$ or 20%      **[1 mark]**

**3** 0      **[1 mark]**

**4** $\dfrac{5}{7}$ or 0.71… or 71%      **[1 mark]**

**5** 2% or 0.02 or $\dfrac{1}{50}$      **[1 mark]**

**6** 0.1 or $\dfrac{1}{10}$ or 10%      **[1 mark]**

**7** $\dfrac{1}{12}$ or 0.083… or 8.3%      **[2 marks]**
**[1 mark]** for working with a denominator of 12

**8** $\dfrac{23}{60}$ or 0.033… or 3.3%      **[2 marks]**

   **[1 mark]** for working with a denominator of 60

# Probability 85: Answers

**1** HH   HT   TH   TT      **[1 mark]**

**2** H1   H2   H3   H4   H5   H6      **[1 mark]**
T1   T2   T3   T4   T5   T6

**3** EA   EP      **[1 mark]**
CA   CP
HA   HP

**4** PB   SB   FB
PC   SC   FC      **[1 mark]**

**5** 2, 3, 4, 5, 6, 7, 8      **[1 mark]**

**6** 0, 1, 2, 3, 4, 5      **[1 mark]**

**7** HHH   HHT   HTH   HTT      **[2 marks]**
THH   THT   TTH   TTT
**[1 mark]** for six or seven correct

**8** SPI   SPB   SFI   SFB   SVI   SVB      **[2 marks]**
NPI   NPD   NFI   NFB   NVI   NVB
**[1 mark]** for at least six correct

# Probability 86: Answers

**1** 31      **[1 mark]**

**2** 18      **[1 mark]**

**3** 7      **[1 mark]**

**4** 4      **[1 mark]**

**5** 3      **[1 mark]**

**6** 13      **[1 mark]**

**7** 24      **[1 mark]**

**8** 9      **[1 mark]**

**9** 15      **[1 mark]**

**10** $\dfrac{9}{31}$ or 0.29 or $\dfrac{\text{student's H}}{\text{student's A}}$      **[1 mark]**

# Probability 87: Answers

**1** 4, 6, 8      **[1 mark]**

**2** 1      **[1 mark]**

**3** 3, 5, 7                     **[1 mark]**

**4** 2                     **[1 mark]**

**5** $\dfrac{1}{2}$                     **[1 mark]**

**6** $\dfrac{3}{8}$                     **[1 mark]**

**7** $\dfrac{3}{8}$

    **[1 mark]** for correct numerator     **[2 marks]**

**8** $\dfrac{1}{8}$

    **[1 mark]** for correct numerator     **[2 marks]**

## Probability 88: Answers

**1** 1, 2, 3                     **[1 mark]**

**2** $\dfrac{2}{3}$                     **[1 mark]**

**3** 1,4  1,5  1,6  1,7
   2,4  2,5  2,6  2,7
   3,4  3,5  3,6  3,7           **[1 mark]**

**4** $\dfrac{1}{3}$                     **[1 mark]**

**5** 4,8  4,9  4,10  4,11  4,12
   5,8  5,9  5,10  5,11  5,12
   6,8  6,9  6,10  6,11  6,12
   7,8  7,9  7,10  7,11  7,12     **[1 mark]**

**6** $\dfrac{1}{4}$                     **[1 mark]**

**7** 1,9  1,10  1,11  1,12
   2,9  2,10  2,11  2,12
   3,9  3,10  3,11  3,12
   1/15                 **[1 mark]**

**8** $\dfrac{1}{15}$                   **[1 mark]**

**9** $\dfrac{1}{30}$

    **[1 mark]** for $\dfrac{1}{3}$, $\dfrac{1}{4}$ and $\dfrac{2}{5}$ seen     **[2 marks]**

## Statistics 89: Answers

**1**

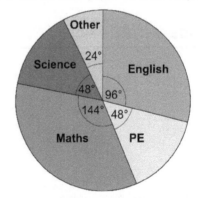

Pictogram to show pupils' favourite subject

English     PE     Maths     Science     Other     Key represents 4 pupils

**[3 marks]** for fully correct pictogram:
**[1 mark]** for title
**[1 mark]** for a key
**[1 mark]** for correct representation     **[3 marks]**

**2**

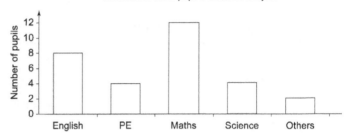

Barchart to show pupil's favourite subject

**[3 marks]** for fully correct bar chart:
**[1 mark]** for title and correctly labelled axes
**[1 mark]** for all correct column heights
**[1 mark]** for correct representation     **[3 marks]**

**3**

Pie chart to show pupils' favourite subject

**[4 marks]** for fully correct pie chart:
**[1 mark]** for title and sectors by subject
**[3 marks]** for all angles correctly
calculated and drawn
**[2 marks]** for at least 3 angles correctly
calculated and drawn
**[1 mark]** for at least 2 angles correctly
calculated     **[4 marks]**

## Statistics 90: Answers

**1** 8                     **[1 mark]**

**2** 9                     **[1 mark]**

**3** 32 **[1 mark]** for 8 + 3 + 12 + 9 seen     **[2 marks]**

**4** Facebook               **[1 mark]**

**5** WhatsApp             **[1 mark]**

**6** 45                        [1 mark]

**7** Answer in range 1320 to      [2 marks]
   1,380 inclusive
   **[1 mark]** for value in range 66 to 69
   inclusive seen

**8** Valid reason e.g. fewer books    [2 marks]
   being borrowed

# Statistics 91: Answers

**1** 13                         [1 mark]

**2** 15 minutes             [1 mark]

**3** 34                         [1 mark]

**4** City B                   [1 mark]

**5** 3                          [1 mark]

**6** 5°C                       [1 mark]

**7** 180                       [1 mark]

**8** 240                       [1 mark]

**9** 210
   **[1 mark]** for 180 + 240 + 90 or 510 or
   360 − (90 + 120 + 45) or 105    [2 marks]

# Statistics 92: Answers

**1** 5                          [1 mark]

**2** 8.5                       [1 mark]

**3** 9                          [1 mark]

**4** 6                          [1 mark]

**5** 12                        [1 mark]

**6** 1.1                       [1 mark]

**7** 2, 10 **[1 mark]** for each value    [2 marks]

**8** 6 **[1 mark]** for e.g. $\dfrac{36 + x}{7}$ seen    [2 marks]

# Statistics 93: Answers

**1** C                         [1 mark]

**2** A                         [1 mark]

**3** B                         [1 mark]

**4** Positive correlation       [1 mark]

**5** L                         [1 mark]

**6** 4                          [1 mark]

**7** G and H **[1 mark]** for each student    [2 marks]

**8** F and H **[1 mark]** for each student    [2 marks]

Name _____     Class _____

## Recall Tests for GCSE 9-1 Maths Record Sheet

| Tests | Mark | Total marks | Attempts | | |
|---|---|---|---|---|---|
| | | | 1st | 2nd | 3rd |
| Number 1 | | 10 | | | |
| Number 2 | | 10 | | | |
| Number 3 | | 10 | | | |
| Number 4 | | 10 | | | |
| Number 5 | | 10 | | | |
| Number 6 | | 10 | | | |
| Number 7 | | 10 | | | |
| Number 8 | | 10 | | | |
| Number 9 | | 10 | | | |
| Number 10 | | 10 | | | |
| Number 11 | | 10 | | | |
| Number 12 | | 10 | | | |
| Number 13 | | 10 | | | |
| Number 14 | | 10 | | | |
| Number 15 | | 10 | | | |
| Number 16 | | 10 | | | |
| Number 17 | | 10 | | | |
| Number 18 | | 10 | | | |
| Number 19 | | 10 | | | |
| Number 20 | | 10 | | | |
| Number 21 | | 10 | | | |
| Number 22 | | 10 | | | |
| Number 23 | | 10 | | | |
| Algebra 24 | | 10 | | | |
| Algebra 25 | | 10 | | | |
| Algebra 26 | | 10 | | | |
| Algebra 27 | | 10 | | | |
| Algebra 28 | | 10 | | | |
| Algebra 29 | | 10 | | | |
| Algebra 30 | | 10 | | | |
| Algebra 31 | | 10 | | | |
| Algebra 32 | | 10 | | | |
| Algebra 33 | | 10 | | | |
| Algebra 34 | | 10 | | | |
| Algebra 35 | | 10 | | | |
| Algebra 36 | | 10 | | | |
| Algebra 37 | | 10 | | | |

Name _____     Class _____

## Recall Tests for GCSE 9-1 Maths Record Sheet

| Tests | Mark | Total marks | Attempts (Marks) | | |
|-------|------|-------------|------|------|------|
| | | | 1st | 2nd | 3rd |
| Algebra 38 | | 10 | | | |
| Algebra 39 | | 10 | | | |
| Algebra 40 | | 10 | | | |
| Algebra 41 | | 10 | | | |
| Algebra 42 | | 10 | | | |
| Algebra 43 | | 10 | | | |
| Algebra 44 | | 10 | | | |
| Algebra 45 | | 10 | | | |
| Algebra 46 | | 10 | | | |
| Algebra 47 | | 10 | | | |
| Ratio, proportion and rates of change 48 | | 10 | | | |
| Ratio, proportion and rates of change 49 | | 10 | | | |
| Ratio, proportion and rates of change 50 | | 10 | | | |
| Ratio, proportion and rates of change 51 | | 10 | | | |
| Ratio, proportion and rates of change 52 | | 10 | | | |
| Ratio, proportion and rates of change 53 | | 10 | | | |
| Ratio, proportion and rates of change 54 | | 10 | | | |
| Ratio, proportion and rates of change 55 | | 10 | | | |
| Ratio, proportion and rates of change 56 | | 10 | | | |
| Ratio, proportion and rates of change 57 | | 10 | | | |
| Ratio, proportion and rates of change 58 | | 10 | | | |
| Ratio, proportion and rates of change 59 | | 10 | | | |
| Ratio, proportion and rates of change 60 | | 10 | | | |
| Ratio, proportion and rates of change 61 | | 10 | | | |
| Geometry and measures 62 | | 10 | | | |
| Geometry and measures 63 | | 10 | | | |
| Geometry and measures 64 | | 10 | | | |
| Geometry and measures 65 | | 10 | | | |
| Geometry and measures 66 | | 10 | | | |
| Geometry and measures 67 | | 10 | | | |
| Geometry and measures 68 | | 10 | | | |
| Geometry and measures 69 | | 10 | | | |
| Geometry and measures 70 | | 10 | | | |
| Geometry and measures 71 | | 10 | | | |
| Geometry and measures 72 | | 10 | | | |
| Geometry and measures 73 | | 10 | | | |
| Geometry and measures 74 | | 10 | | | |

Name _____     Class _____

## Recall Tests for GCSE 9-1 Maths Record Sheet

| Tests | Mark | Total marks | Attempts (Marks) | | |
|---|---|---|---|---|---|
| | | | 1st | 2nd | 3rd |
| Geometry and measures 75 | | 10 | | | |
| Geometry and measures 76 | | 10 | | | |
| Geometry and measures 77 | | 10 | | | |
| Geometry and measures 78 | | 10 | | | |
| Geometry and measures 79 | | 10 | | | |
| Geometry and measures 80 | | 10 | | | |
| Geometry and measures 81 | | 10 | | | |
| Geometry and measures 82 | | 10 | | | |
| Probability 83 | | 10 | | | |
| Probability 84 | | 10 | | | |
| Probability 85 | | 10 | | | |
| Probability 86 | | 10 | | | |
| Probability 87 | | 10 | | | |
| Probability 88 | | 10 | | | |
| Statistics 89 | | 10 | | | |
| Statistics 90 | | 10 | | | |
| Statistics 91 | | 10 | | | |
| Statistics 92 | | 10 | | | |
| Statistics 93 | | 10 | | | |

**Recall Tests for GCSE 9-1 Maths Record Sheet**